ATTENTION AND CREATION

ATTENTION AND CREATION
Growth in the Vertices of W.R. Bion

Fin Egenfeldt-Nielsen

Routledge
Taylor & Francis Group
LONDON AND NEW YORK

First published 2010 by Karnac Books Ltd.

2 Park Square, Milton Park, Abingdon, Oxfordshire OX14 4RN
52 Vanderbilt Avenue, New York, NY 10017

Routledge is an imprint of the Taylor & Francis Group, an informa business

First issued in hardback 2019

British Library Cataloguing in Publication Data

A C.I.P. for this book is available from the British Library

ISBN-13: 978-1-85575-653-3 (pbk)
ISBN-13: 978-0-367-32339-4 (hbk)

Typeset by Vikatan Publishing Solutions (P) Ltd., Chennai, India

CONTENTS

ACKNOWLEDGMENTS

I would like to express my deepest gratitude to Karen and Barry D. Proner. I will be indebted to them till the day I die for their warm generosity and deep insights.

Likewise, Dr Jes Bertelsen has been teacher and instructor to me at every level of awareness and academia. I am eternally grateful.

Through their practice as therapists and supervisors, Søren Aagaard, Ejgil Nyborg, Anne Halveg, Hans Henrik Hoff and Thorkild Sørensen have enabled me to grow as a person and a therapist. Little would have succeeded without their attention and their patience.

The many analysands and pupils who have trusted me have taught me more than I had ever thought possible. Their courage and devotion have shown me that the way into myself was possible and necessary. Though I cannot list them by name, they are in my heart.

Many have contributed to the present form of this paper. Of utmost importance was the proofreading of my two translators Karen and Caitlín, of the Danish manuscript, and discussions with Lenni Kari, and her keen interest and sharp scrutiny. So many errors were detected. For all those that remain I beg the reader's indulgence.

ABOUT THE AUTHOR

Fin Egenfeldt-Nielsen is a psychotherapist working in private practice in Troense and Copenhagen, Denmark.

In his youth he earned degrees in history and philosophy, which he taught at high school and university until 1998.

From 1980 to 2001 he worked in several publicly subsidized but privately run institutions for disadvantaged children and young people. This work took place partly from his home and partly on sailboats where the young people lived and worked with adults as part of a controlled community, enabling them to adjust to the demands of adult life while working on their academic skills and—more importantly—the skills required to look after themselves.

From 1987 to 1998 he trained as a Jungian analyst in London and Copenhagen, where disagreements with individual Jungian analysts in Copenhagen led to a painful break with the Society of Analytical Psychology of Copenhagen, which was to prove an opportunity for learning and personal growth.

He studied psychology at the Open University in Roskilde between 1995 and 1996, earning a diploma in psychoanalysis in 2004 from the Psychotherapeutic Working Group on Funen. He has been a member of the Ethics Committee of the Danish Association for Psychotherapists (Psykoterapeut Foreningen) since 2000, and chairman of the Board of the Educational Committee since 2008.

INTRODUCTION

> The mind that does not understand is the Buddha: There is no other.
>
> (Suzuki, 2008, p. 57)

Wilfred Rupert Bion was born in India in 1897. He died in England in 1979 shortly after deciding to return to India once again, feeling that this country had been a strong inspiration to him in his work. His world-view is moulded by the stories from the Mahābhārata which his Indian nurse told him and which pervade the ontological and epistemological theories that characterise his psychoanalytic thought, i.e.:

1. His concept of God or the Godhead, i.e., "O".
2. His rationalist empiricism that was framed by Platonic idealism and Kantian empiricism while qualitatively determined by an Indian world-view insisting on consciousness as an active organ that may be altered and developed through use. The key to Bion's own vein of phenomenology lies in this fusion of otherwise contradictory theories of knowledge—rationalism and empiricism.

3. His monism or transcendental ontology that attributes to the mind its own being and space.
4. His belief in the mind as an active organ, to be altered and developed through the consumption of reality in the form of thought. This may be understood as a reinterpretation of Kant's transcendental deductions on reason since Bion identifies reason as being active and creative, both internally vis-à-vis the mind in and of itself, and externally vis-à-vis reality. Furthermore, the mind—be it individual or collective—is formed through both ontogenesis and phylogenesis.

Perhaps the most remarkable facet of Bion's personality was his courage in seeking truth without being preoccupied with results. For him, it was always the questions that were important—never the answers. Bion considered answers a form of passing illness, a kind of lie; an attitude reminiscent of Freud and other significant thinkers, scientists or mystics who shared this ability to create something out of nothing or "O".

In this sense, Bion aligns himself with 20th century phenomenological, existential and hermeneutic thought. The psychoanalysis Bion exposed at his supervisory seminars in the 1970s, particularly those held in South America, embraces clinical work that seeks to heal the rifts in the meta-theories of psychoanalysis that emerged during the early years of psychoanalysis, when school after school split off. Thus Bion is a kind of Newton or Kant of psychotherapy and the generalisation of meta-theory expressed in his "Grid" constitutes a framework of conceptual spaces for forms of mind.

Perhaps Bion's thought enables an understanding of the differences between various therapeutic schools, as more a question of differences in style than of actually contradictory systems, and the utilisation and usefulness of the various schools becomes a function of the personality of the therapist and the needs of the analysand.

Certainly we know more than we can express and much more than we can put to meaningful use in clinical work.

Bion's almost idealistic insistence on intuition, creativity, openness and attentiveness in therapeutic sessions can thus be said to recreate the world phenomenologically and existentially in each encounter and in each session through the language invented by the two individuals involved in order to express feelings, emotions and sensations. Therapy is a non-theoretical meeting. Thoughts before and after a session are theoretical and meta-theoretical considerations that may or may not result in a shower of worthless publications. Significance lies in the attentive atmosphere of the session itself.

This work is no exception but may—hopefully—provide the reader with a laugh rather than entrenchment or blockades between factions.

The vital importance of Bion's role in psychoanalysis—similar to those of Freud, Klein and Jung—lies perhaps in the fact that Bion's overarching goal is to designate a shared frame of reference for work with consciousness or for the analysis of consciousness, psychoanalysis, analytical psychology, psychotherapy and the like.

In 1995, Michael Fordham—a central figure in analytical psychology and the editor of C.G. Jung's collected works in English and in his late eighties at the time—published a book which I consider in some ways a psychoanalyst's will (Fordham, 1995, pp. 69–75.).[1] In a private conversation I had with him about this book, I asked him for his opinion on the controversies between the Zürich and London schools of analytical psychology. My question was emotionally loaded, having trained in London and about to live and work in Copenhagen I felt that maybe I had positioned myself precariously on the fence. His answer was the equally loaded, "I could not care less".

I believe that this remark reflected his belief that therapy emanates from each therapist's individually acquired and created mind-form.[2] All roads of sufficient intensity and will power emanate from and lead to the same goal: We walk in solitude and we arrive alone. The insight that we need to proceed is that there must be no fences between those who sincerely attempt to reach togetherness with another.

In order to reach this goal it is necessary to break down—in both senses of the word—and remove the (de)fences to lay out the mind for common grazing. This is precisely what Bion sought to accomplish through generalisations and abstractions—most clearly exemplified in the "Grid"—to create a common of pasture for human individuals, both analysts and analysands. Indeed, for humans.

This book has four main chapters. Chapter One is a brief introduction to Bion himself. Since I assume a certain degree of familiarity with his life and work, I have included only what I consider essential to understanding the work on which this book is centred.

Chapter Two is an explication of the main thesis, demonstrating how Bion articulates his theories and systems of the transformation of the immaterial elements, which constitute the psyche.

Chapter Three elucidates views on therapeutic techniques, my own and those of Bion. Touching on the routes available to those wishing to become therapists it also discusses the demands this may place on those in a position to help, be they teachers, supervisors or more experienced fellow therapists.

Chapter Four has two parts: the first outlines Bion's conceptual framework for the constitution, capture and systematisation of psychic space and the elements hereof; the second details a series of classic, mythical attempts at similar processes exemplified in the stories of Oedipus, Original Sin, Palinurus, and the Tower of Babel.

The implicit background of this book consists of the more optimistic approaches to creating mindforms that improve the conditions of humanity which derive from the legends of Christ and the Buddha and the experiences of mystics in both Eastern and Western cultures, as well as from psychoanalytic thought to which I am obviously indebted.

Notes

1. The conflict concerned mostly the significance of the unconscious, transference, and attachment, and their theoretical and clinical status. The main post-Jungian schools were the "archetypal school", based in Zürich, and "the developmental" or "clinical" school—in which the significance of "the here and now" between the therapist and analyst/analysand was highly valued—based in London (see also Samuels 1985, p. 94).
2. The concept of mindform.

CHAPTER ONE

Bion: Man and mystic

In 1905, Bion left India, the country of his birth and early childhood, to arrive in England, aged eight years old. He only saw his mother a few times after this point, but his father came to live with him in London after her death. He entered the army at 17 and after engaging actively in a war whose terrors left him marked for life, he was decorated for his courage. There can be little doubt that Bion suffered from PTSD; this is perhaps most clearly felt in his literary work *A Memoir of the Future*. His military prowess and his conspicuous rugby talent gained him access to Oxford University, however, since he did not consider himself to be possessed of much intelligence, he chose to study history; a subject he assumed he could manage. Graduating in 1921 he taught history until he was turned away in 1924 after being accused of child molestation, charges he vehemently denied. He then went on to study medicine, graduating in 1929. In the late 1930s he began his analytical training by undergoing analysis with John Rickmann but was interrupted by World War II, where he worked with wounded officers who were required to return to the front as quickly as possible and assisted Rickmann in selecting officers for active service. After the war he continued his work at Tavistock, undergoing analysis with Melanie Klein. During this period his working experiences led him to develop his group theories—a form of work psychology or social psychology describing the inner dynamics of collective phenomena.

Bion lost his first wife during the birth of his daughter Parthenope in 1945. He remarried six years later and had two children by his second wife.

Bion himself, probably the most original thinker since Freud, claims not to have formulated anything particularly original. In my opinion this is not so much a question of modesty as an acknowledgment of the indebtedness of all thought to that, which has previously been formulated. Moreover, Bion claims that all thought is present and finds the thinker; Plato, Descartes, Kant and Freud were found as he himself is attempting to be found. All that is required of thinkers is to open themselves up to the myriad of thoughts, as flowers open up to bees in order to be pollinated. Naturally, hard work ensues from this point.

After completing psychoanalysis with Melanie Klein, Bion obtained almost cult-like stature in the psychoanalytical world of the late 1940s. It seems likely that he left England for San Francisco in order to escape this attention. He does not seem to have settled in the U.S. however, but continued to South America, where he found the peace and acceptance that allowed him to express his thoughts in their most "user-friendly" form.

Bion's professional work can be divided as follows:

1. Groups
2. Psychotic patients
3. Formulation of a meta-scientific frame of reference for psychoanalysis.

To Bion, psychoanalysis is the work of seeking to stimulate psychic growth: it is also the soul's path to truth, wholeness, freedom, unity or "O". All transformations take place in this principally indefinable "O" to which all paths eventually lead. These transformations are development or growth before becoming the solid psychic forms that we call habit, prejudice, personality, culture, etc. The truth is what the mystic knows, not the relative truths known to science, whose precision may at best be described as paralleled by their brevity.

Thus the way forward for Bion was that of the mystic, the spiritual path described for instance by St. John of the Cross in his poem The Dark Night of the Soul: a fundamental polarity unfolding between the mystic and the establishment, where the mystic seeks the truth while the establishment possesses it—at least in a relative sense. This relative truth is expressed culturally, socially and psychically through laws, regulations, norms and forms of consciousness as well as through works of art and interpretations of "nature". This relative and changeable "truth" features overlying structures like personality types, pathology, normality, science and technology. The establishment functions when this group opens to mysticism, creating changes in the framework of un-freedom in which mysticism exists—so to speak in captivity. But everyone—including the individual—functions when alertly developing, either throughout their own life processes or through therapeutic courses. The establishment becomes a container adapting to the contents of the truth created by the mystic, but each individual is also adapting to this deep truth through his or her own individual life process of moving towards freedom. There is a kind of container/contained "♂♀" between the individual and a movement "Ps<=>D".[1]

The concept of an "act of faith" is a central issue, one expressed both in the analyst's meeting with the analysand and in the individual's meeting with the group. For when instinct, or whatever is presented to the conscious mind in this meeting, is interpreted sometimes narcissistically[2] sometimes socially[3] the individual or the group believe that their survival may best be ensured in accordance with the dominant psychic structure at the moment of presentation. When this structure is narcissistic the group is resisted whereas if it is social, the individual follows the group. From a psychotic point of view the individual will disappear and split.[4] This means that in the case of narcissistic love, any hatred will target the group, while in the case of socially oriented love, hatred will target the individual, and when love is absent hatred will target the self or awareness.[5] The ego constitutes the connection between external and internal realities, thus mediating between love and hatred in relation to both the group and the self. With the dissolution of memory, desire, understanding and expectation, this mediating ego is also dissolved, the mystic obtains truth and the soul sees the light as the darkest night.[6]

The opportunity for development lies in the constant repetition of this process.

William Blake describes this beautifully:

> He who binds to himself a joy
> Doth the winged life destroy
> But he who kisses the joy as it flies
> Lives in Eternitys sun rise.
>
> (Blake, 2004, p. 158)

Here, however, we also have the possibility of negative development, a kind of "misguided" growth, dominated by inhibitions and defensive positions, where trust, faith and gratitude are weak, while anxiety and envy are strong. This "misguided growth" is described in several Old Testament myths. In the story of original sin the unhappy consequences are described as the wrath of God descending on Adam and Eve when they purloin fruit the Tree of Knowledge. The Tower of Babel tells a cautionary tale of what may happen when humans seek to reach divine heights. The content and form of every myth indicate possibilities of both negative and positive developments, as I try to describe it in the chapters on symbols, models and analogies.

Bion lived through the wartime destruction of World War I. His experiences condensed around the traumatizing events that took place under the battle of Amiens, where he saw the soldier next to him get his head blown off and found himself one of only a few survivors. These experiences come back to him day and night and I think that this was what led him to acknowledge that life arises in the shadow of death. He may perhaps at this moment experience what Sabina Spielrein terms "destruction as a cause of coming into being" (Spielrein, 1994, p. 155). Life survives all destruction, but all must also be destroyed in order to persist. The terror that this thought inspires holds the openness necessary for development. Here—in this gap—there is only the act of faith. This is "O".

Through his life's work, Bion indicated that there are vast areas of the human psyche—both at the individual and the collective levels—full of unknown suffering, and that these threaten our survival both as individuals and as a species. Psychoanalysis, art and music try to reach these areas to bring relief and prevent them from triggering destructive processes on a larger scale. We witness these destructive areas on a small scale every day, in and amongst ourselves as well as others. Psychoanalysis attempts to reach these areas through language in a meeting that seeks to transform the barbarian and the barbaric through empathy and identification. In this process the analysand contributes the material to be transformed, allowing the analyst to be cured (of his or her stupidity or barbarousness) and perhaps to cure. This process creates existence or perhaps just creates.

Bion's demonstration that the psyche of each and every person is reflected in the psyche of each and every other is pivotal. Thus there is only one psyche, folding and unfolding in each individual like a hologram while at the same time partaking of humankind. To realize this is to realize the necessity of empathy. Bion saw this in the learning that passes between mother and child and that later always serves as a connecting link to a shared human apperception. Thus Bion also indicated the enormous capacity of the psyche for adaptation, change and empathy, in other words its ability to develop and grow.

Perhaps Bion's opus reflects his own individual psychic development; perhaps it reflects the collective psychic development of our age. Perhaps his work is a "snapshot" of our psyche, just as *Oedipus Rex* and *Oedipus at Colonos* were snapshots of the psyche 2500 years ago.

Notes

1. Spinoza expresses this beautifully by showing how true freedom is the realisation of the necessary in the form of the true, the virtuous, and the beautiful.
2. That is to say, when my self, perhaps my false self, is in focus.
3. Here the self or a more collective self is in focus. Ideally, a human community is the goal.
4. According to Bion, psychosis is a condition in which the ability of the individual to think is destroyed, perhaps even eliminated.
5. Most people know this condition best in its modified form as envy.
6. It is the goal of this text to offer a sort of understanding of this special kind of creativity in therapy.

CHAPTER TWO

Theory

I am blind because I see too much. That's why I read by a dark lamp.

(Theilgaard, 1995, p. 166)

a. What are psychoanalytic development, change and growth?

Theories, myths, symbols and concepts are used in therapy not because they are true, false or significant, but because they are part of a motion towards truth, when this movement is positive. This motion, implicitly towards greater freedom and capacity for love is the only form of development or growth in the psychoanalytic sense. But development may be negative or even destructive, i.e., moving towards lies, un-freedom, or force. Psychotherapy is a tool or guide in this search for truth. Such pursuit is a form of religious activity because truth is always transcendental in character. Truth is—so to speak—not of this world. Our theories change. We do not know if they become better or truer, but what happens in therapy—an activity taking place in the now, in the therapist-analysand dyad—is a truth towards which we may be more or less accurately attentive.

Psychoanalysis or therapy is an activity, a piece of reality. When psychoanalysis or therapy is science, it is the science of this particular piece of reality. Hence psychoanalytical science is empirical and like all empirical science it has a theoretical life of its own, subject to the same demands as other empirical sciences. Just as a ballistic mathematical formula is useful when it brings its subject to the desired goal, so theories on therapy are useful when they bring the therapist and the analysand closer to the truth, and as Kierkegaard says: the truth is always subjective (Kierkegaard, 1925). Subjectivity and objectivity merge or lose their significance when there is no possibility of reaching that, which lies outside the psyche. Psychoanalytical science is in some ways similar to historical science, in that it also deals with that which is lost forever, i.e., the past and the attempt to recreate this lost past through the activities of the historian. Indeed it is said that each generation of historians must create its own understanding of the past. Similarly each generation of therapists must create their own image both of the individual and the collective. Every therapeutic sequence recreates both analyst and analysand. Bion might have said that this would ideally happen in every session, in each individual moment.

This view of science claims that the science of therapy does tend to—in fact, must—approximate the nature of the true human and that the truth can never be fully known, nor should it be. This applies to every science. Yet the activity that is therapy creates and unfolds truth, i.e., the subjective truth that is always present in the moment unfolding between therapist and analysand. This act of creation is the existential precondition and the consciousnesses and bodies at work in the course of therapy are at once created and existent through this work. Naturally this same process may take place in the course of any life. Therapy merely attempts to speed up the process.

Empirical sciences are defined by the partial realities they examine. Psychoanalysis examines consciousness. We do not know what consciousness is until we create the languages or scientific theories to describe it, just as we understand little of reality as a whole prior to creating language or theories to describe it. Bion's work is a quest for such a language of consciousness. In principle, research into psychoanalytic or empirical consciousness is no different from other empirical areas of research; to each its own field, complete with methods and techniques. In other empirical sciences, the observer and the observed mutually affect each other—a phenomenon particularly evident in microphysics—thus also in psychoanalysis. Perhaps the degree of this mutuality is more pronounced and significant in psychoanalysis, necessitating other types of methods and techniques, but in every scientific context, the choice of method and technique is a significant factor in determining what goals are reached.

Freud believed that consciousness was a special organ. Thus our senses consist of sight, hearing, smell, taste, touch and thought, where thought relates to those psychic qualities and quantities that constitute the "matter" or fields of research into psychoanalysis and consciousness. Bion expresses this by claiming that thoughts are to the thinker as matter, waves, particles etc., in their various forms are to the other senses. Bion calls the capacity for thought "Oedipus" in his first drafts of a theory of consciousness. "Oedipus" thus becomes the sign or symbol of a quest for thoughts to think about.

I believe that it may be expedient or practical to refer to a specific space for these psychic objects. This special space can perhaps be understood as unfolding from or of the ordinary Euclidian space of height, width, depth and time. Here the psyche is charted in both a phylogenetic and ontogenetic perspective. Bion attempted to map this space using concepts he gathered in what he calls the "Grid", which he considers to be a kind of tool, perhaps a kind of system of referral for elements of consciousness, just as a system of co-ordinates is a system of referral for, e.g., algebraic equations, or the movement of physical objects like the Sun or the planets through space.

In brief, people share psychic space just as they share Euclidian space. Both spaces together constitute the universe and feature their own separate accumulations of matter, their own galaxies and black holes. It has been claimed that the "Grid" is to psychoanalysis what the periodic table is to chemistry. Its space is defined by the coordinates Love/Hate, +/−Knowledge and a series of functions that Bion calls Paranoid schizoid <=> Depressive, container/contained, projective identification, alpha-function, and reverie. It is also within this space that we find Bion's beta elements, bizarre elements, alpha elements, object relations, objects, and archetypical structures or schemata.

Movements within this space in a shared time are what we term development. Many philosophers have wondered whether it would make sense to discuss a Euclidian space in time if there were no people to formulate such a thought. Similarly it is possible to question whether it is possible to refer to psychic space without humankind. I mention this only to emphasize the existential parallels between the physical and the psychic sciences.

I find it reasonable to introduce these ideas in relation to this topic since it is necessary, if we are to discuss development, change and growth, to determine a space in which these things can happen. Thus by logical necessity there is a place, a space for therapy, and we know that when we are in a therapy setting, intensely at work, the physical space and usual time around us disappear to be replaced by psychic space and the objects populating it. The relationship between therapist and analysand is the decisive aspect in this moment, where everything disappears. Bion calls it "xKy" and indicates that this relation may only be understood in relation to the excluded third (party) in the form of the "supervisor/group of colleagues/humankind". This space is positioned in both relations and as physical space is a common space, so is psychic space. Bion also believes that development and growth can take place through insight only at this moment, defined as the "now" in which thought finds its thinker. This can happen only when the thinker is in a state of "no memory, no desire, no understanding, no expectation" (Bion, 1992, pp. 380–385). The development to be sought moves towards the depressive state of consciousness[1] that holds and thereby expresses the complexity of existence, unlike the splitting, polarizing and fragmenting effect of the paranoid-schizoid on our interior and exterior reality. Like Melanie Klein, Bion believes that our consciousness swings from a depressive to a paranoid-schizoid condition, a belief he expresses using the "formula" or symbol "Ps<=>D". The arrows emphasize the fact that this development is a shift between directions. This applies both collectively and individually and both in a species-historical and individual-historical perspective. I perceive the development towards D as an upward motion towards goodness, reality and a greater degree of freedom.

The movement may thus be upwards or downwards for the individual, the species and the collective. During the 1930s, we experienced a downward motion, as is the case right now. It is easy to see that the paranoid-schizoid condition of both individuals and groups was augmented during the rise of Fascism in the 1930s. This is now happening again in the collision between the secularized, power-seeking versions of the Islamic and Christian faiths.

In the years following the bombing of Hiroshima in August 1945, awareness of the physical place or "now" changed. We understood that we were in this together. The bombing of Hiroshima polluted Siberia; a bomb over Moscow scared Europe, just as the thought of a bomb over Iceland scared New Yorkers etc., Suddenly we shared physical space. Now it is evident that psychic space is shared as well. The schizoid position of an Iranian leader can be reproduced in heads-of-government in the West and vice versa, which is no more remarkable than the transference that takes place in a therapeutic setting. After all, it is one space.

The direction towards a depressive position, i.e., an accommodating position, entails positive developments, change and growth. There is life first in the development of the ego, then in individuation or self-development. Knowledge is acquired, perhaps insight; the pursuit of which is the most pronounced religious—or perhaps one should say, meaning- and status-imbuing—activity, except perhaps for the dance around the golden calf. However, in psychic space, knowledge—which in Euclidian space seems positive—can turn out to be negative. For example, the terms growth and development are used within the field of biology, where growth can generate more, bigger, prettier, but also poorer foodstuffs, pumped with water, nitrite and artificial fertilizers; the exploitation of the earth, etc. Perhaps something similar takes place in therapy.

Like modern personalities, modern society may be characterized as narcissistic. The problems we encounter as therapists are basically an expression of a warped attachment to warped values. We express the cry for help of our unbalanced psychic lives through our abuse, just as the surroundings to which we are attached scream too. Nature plays Echo to our Narcissus. We swing from devaluing, deflating notions, dreams and levels to inflated notions of grandeur depending on our mood. Like the humble and self-repressed, the arrogant and conceited are prey to greed, envy or jealousy. When these "deadly sins" function as active social or psychic structures or dominant traits, growth is "misguided". Society and we ourselves are in the throes of insanity and this particular kind of insanity paralyzes our ability to think and thus to acknowledge our deranged condition. Our intellect is fragmented (Symington, 2007).

In Euripides' 5th century BCE tragedy *The Bacchae*, Dionysus strikes Agave, mother of Pentheus and daughter of Cadmus, with insanity to punish her for her conceit. In her ravings she rips her son apart and puts his head on a stake as a hunting trophy. Triumphantly, she enters the city, where Cadmus succeeds in making her see herself with all the attending pain and horror this insight causes.

Some forms of therapy may produce a kind of "misguided" growth; perhaps this is the form of therapy that aims to return the individual to the factory at any cost, even when this cost is not in accordance with the individual's own deeper layers and desires for value and meaning. Therapy then becomes non-development for both therapist and analysand. These are therapeutic forms that lead to adaptation, functional efficiency and personal un-freedom.

A good gardener prunes trees not only to make them grow, but to make them strong and beautiful. A good-enough mother is precisely the bad-enough mother.

The question is whether this is a new insight, or whether our scientific theories are dealing with ancient myths dressed up in modern scientific language; a new choreography of the dance around the golden calf?

Yet the desperation that often appears to characterize our search for the truth, which degenerates into a wild goose chase, indicates that we must find new ways to survive and new mindforms. This seems to be an ultimate objective of therapy.

In short, "Psychotherapy" *equals* "search for truth" *equals* "development/change/growth" *equals* "freedom". Psychoanalysis is practice (Grinberg 1990, p. 161), i.e., movement between paranoid-schizoid and depressive states, and positive development means moving towards the depressive state, i.e., towards that which holds contradictions and complexity.

Psychoanalytic and other meta-theories like science, theory, technique, and forms stand in contrast to this, but then psychoanalysis termed psi column in Bion's "Grid" is fallacious, because it is not real, just as a nautical map is not the sea itself.

Schools of therapy

Psychoanalysis is generally considered to be a form of therapy, treatment, or practice, which is meta-theoretically founded. It is one of many schools of therapy, each with its own respective groups of therapists and analysands. The task here is to match these many groups in order to maximize creativity and growth. An open, respectful attitude to the intuitions of consciousness is decisive in this respect.

Polarisations between different groups who consider themselves to be "establishment" are counterproductive and an expression of "misguided growth" with all the splitting, power-struggle, anxiety and envy this engenders. All forms of therapy are related and the history of its individual forms goes a long way back, beyond Oedipus and the interpretations of the great transformational epics like *Gilgamesh*, *Tamuz*, and the *Bhagavad Gita*, as well as Mithraic and Christian legends. Basically existential, experience-oriented, cognitive, Jungian, Freudian and systemic gestalt-therapy are mnemonic tools to assist navigation in unfamiliar waters. We must abandon the fences between the different therapeutic schools in order to verbalize the differences. Cultural development takes place through intermarriage and visiting between friends as well as strangers. Those who are entirely unknown must also be brought into dialogue in order to facilitate the exchange of information.

b. What are psychoanalytic concepts of development, change and growth not?

Within the fields of philosophy, history and biology, the concept of development has enjoyed a revival in recent centuries. Most people are familiar with the theories of Darwin and Lamarck on the development of humankind as species and individual, and many have heard of Gibbon, Spengler and Toynbee and their references to the almost biological way in which cultures blossom and die. Biology, geology and physics have also contributed more-or-less occult theories like the Big Bang. These fields have given rise to a number of techniques for instigating change, e.g., animal husbandry and DNA-manipulation. Essentially, these theories of change and growth have slowly led to a dominating theoretical field that excludes qualitative elements, considering growth only in terms of quantity. This precludes any meaningful reflection on scientific development. Bluntly put, pure positivist science can only produce anti-knowledge, backtracking or "misguided growth".

Cosmogony theories that include qualitative aspects are known from Hesiod's poem, *The Works and Days*, from roughly 500 BCE on the ages of gold-, silver-, and bronze. Qualitatively defined cosmogonies with detailed training programmes are also known from various monastic movements, Gnostic theories of development and from alchemy, and of course from poetry, where e.g., Dante, Goethe, Melville and Dostoyevsky describe the qualitative growth of consciousness or the soul.

Numerous other abstract narratives or theories of development with accompanying training systems in the form of instructions on achieving spiritual growth arose in the great agrarian cultures, in the cults surrounding Inanna, Ishtar and Isis, where transformation arose through ritual unions with Demuzi, Tammuz or Osiris. These action-oriented theories of development or creation are probably some of the profound sources we have on consciousness-transforming work before psychoanalysis and prior to or contemporary with the Indian training systems, which I shall not go into here, merely stating that they are fully functional and still developing to this day.

Thus the search for truth or freedom that is the essence of psychoanalytic practice—and thereby an expression of development or growth—is but one of a number of expressions of human endeavour as they has presumably always existed, leaving specific testimonials, both in our consciousness of today and in the traces of the work they have generated. During the 20th century not only Freud, but also C.G. Jung (in his monumental work *Mysterium Coniunctionis*), and Erich Neumann (in *The Great Mother* and *The Origins and History of Consciousness*) attempted to describe the development or growth of the psyche. Bion's theoretical work seeks a set of "starting-blocks" for this development and in therapeutic sessions everyone participates in this search. Perhaps each individual session can best be described as a "starting block".

Existing developmental theories distinguish between quantitative and qualitative, circular and linear, as well as gradualist or catastrophic change, while also organising development into schematic periods. Psychoanalysis considers growth or change in all these ways, while working within at least two scientific paradigms.

One, which I call the causal paradigm, has causal explanation, control and prognosis as its main objectives, while the other—the dynamic or field paradigm—has insight as its main objective. Insight then, may be that knowledge which is meaningful in and of itself, i.e., knowledge contained in emotions that are existentially affirmative to the collective as well as the individual aspects of humanity. Thereby insight becomes knowledge of the self. I do not quite know what other name to give that into which insight is gained—but nor do I know the nature of the self. Perhaps one might term it "O" in the spirit of Bion himself, or "Christ" as did Jung, or "Brahman/Athman" like the Hindus, or following the Buddhists, the "Buddha nature of the mind". New research on consciousness describes this as a higher level of consciousness, cosmic consciousness, unified consciousness or oneness, or the sixth and seventh level of consciousness (Bertelsen, 1983; 2003, Rinpoche, 1995).

The causal paradigm operates with well-defined schemata like those in developmental psychology, which distinguishes between oral—perhaps primary—narcissistic, symbiotic or autistic, and anal and genital construction. These schemata—which in principle go back to Freud's fascinating and deeply original concept of an oral, anal and genital structure that sediments during childhood—are expanded and modified within the same paradigm in the developmental psychologies of both Piaget and Erikson. They too consider the mind to be constructed during distinct periods that constitute the basis for later thought and action. Statements are true or false and may often be quite easily quantified and compared within a classical scientific-mathematical paradigm. Development has a beginning, middle, and end. This paradigm is wonderful because it provides great peace and security. Within this paradigm knowledge is in a way the closest we can get to the stable world of ideas envisioned by Plato. We also encounter it in simplified descriptive systems like the ICD 10 (the International Classification of Diseases from 1990) or the periodic table of the elements, which captures a range of atomic structure.[2] The mesh of these "nets" is so fine—as is a great deal of knowledge within this paradigm—that we almost as lay-people believe that reality is nothing but what is captured within their weave, that our concepts or "nets" are sufficient to comprehensively describe reality.

Causality is often understood as the most desirable or perhaps even the only expression of scientific insight. This creates focus on the testing of theories through controlled experiments, preferably of a quantifiable nature, and the therapeutic dialogue that takes place in the chaotic everyday reality of the clinic loses significance as a source of insight. Thus the models and qualitative descriptions that best describe clinical situations are rejected as unscientific, although such situations can often be described by simple theoretical systems that fulfil a significant therapeutic purpose by simply creating meaning. It is interesting to note that Aristotle perceived mathematics as the only true science, since it was completely free of "contact" with the chaos and inconstancy of reality. The attainment of empirical knowledge and experience drawing on an interior or exterior reality were relegated to the same, inconstant status. Hence these could not be considered relevant to the search for truth that is the particular hallmark of science.[3] Later the term science itself has—in English—come to refer mainly to natural science, effectively narrowing and impoverishing our modes of experience, and potentially damaging our health. Perhaps the particular material boom we are currently experiencing and the corresponding depletion of non-material values express a kind of psychotic flight from insight vis-à-vis our internal reality with its pain, suffering and anxiety.

One aspect of this reality might be that psychic pain is somatised or converted into physical pain, which appears easier to bear and work with at this point in time. Somatisation is the deposition or projection of psychic material in- or onto the body through an unknown "technique". This means that we do not know how it happens; only that it does. Projection is a "technique" that we have at our disposal for getting rid of what is psychically undesirable or unbearable; again, we do not know how it happens. Other people or groups are transformed—like the body—into vessels for unbearable feelings or psychic pain. Once again we know that it occurs, but not how. While people—as often happens—unwittingly receive and identify with that which is projected—a mechanism known as projective identification. These projections—sometimes poisonous—can and must be returned. The difficulty lies in discovering the poison, regardless of whether its effects are pleasant or noisome.

Within this paradigm, language aims at objects or at achievements, purchases, and action, and is perceived as the language of science. It is pleasure-seeking and positive, prioritizing any form of gratification of psychic needs for security and control, as well as physical needs. The emptiness, nothingness or sparseness of reality, what Bion calls its "no-breast" character, is denied (Bion, 1965, p. 54). In this paradigm we know, think, discover, own, and problem solve. We do not think about thought, there is no "non-being" coupled with a "being", no "I know" coupled with "I do not know". Psychic and physical reality, thought and hallucination, love and hate are not considered two sides of the same coin.

The dynamic paradigm, which I prefer to call the field paradigm, presumes that nothing has a beginning, middle or end; there is no stable order. In this paradigm the world is compared to that river in which we know one cannot bathe twice, for it is always in motion and hence never the same. It is suited to describing the spaces and contents of psychoanalytic reality, in which it is evident that the same two individuals never meet twice.

In this space a different language is at play than in the causal paradigm, which centres attention on itself rather than seeking gain or achievement. Within this linguistic framework the chosen forms of communication are myth, image, narrative, analogy, poetry, music, and mathematics. It uses paradoxes such as the principles of secondary and primary processes that are unified in the consciousness of psychic reality. However, there are also other areas in which this linguistic framework is the most useful. Thus we speak of common sense, of instincts of life and death united in the fact of life, love and hate. We experience and describe the fact of creativity in coitus, in conception and in the movement Ps<=>D. The polarities of Ps and D are united in the fact that we do have a psychic life. Polarity finds another, linguistic expression in the body/spirit dualism, which is united in the real person/the individual itself, as is gender polarity, united both in the concept of the human and in real terms in the psychic world of each individual.[4] Bion's fruitful, therapeutic conceptualization of container and contained finds expression in numerous linguistic, psychic and intra-psychic realities. Concept is articulated in relations like mother/child, analyst/analysand, coupling, *coniunctio*, Samantabhadra and his consort Samantabhadri, and naturally in descriptions of these relations. This paradigm permits moments through dyads, in therapy and in relations both external and internal. These are moments of a particular attention, of existential presence, and potentially of real learning. Such learning is creative and creation (Bion, 1970).

Recently a large number of researchers have begun to approach an understanding, where developmental psychology now matches the "field paradigm". This has also happened in light of the insights that neuropsychology has contributed to psychoanalysis.[5]

Both paradigms may be compared to optic systems or lenses through which reality is at once created and observed; "vertices" or whorls of a sort, in Bion's vivid terms, underlining the fact that our knowledge is determined by the way in which it is gathered.

Sophocles wrote two dramas featuring Oedipus: the young Sophocles wrote *Oedipus Rex* (429 BCE), while *Oedipus at Colonos* (406 BCE) is a mature work. These two dramas may illustrate two stages of consciousness; that of the young Oedipus is grandiose and hence generally psychotically dominated, whereas the more mature Oedipus visiting Colonos has a deeper recognition of his inner reality and is therefore able to achieve a truer, more flexible orientation in his outer world. Thus the two dramas seem to illustrate two "vertices" or two different lenses through which to view the world.

Oedipus Rex

1. A simple response to a complicated problem (sign; lacking comprehension of symbols).
2. Rationality as a yardstick (+/− K).
3. Dependency on the prophetic seer—analyst.
4. Language centring focusing, concentration on the dualities of health/illness, normal/abnormal, pure/impure, cleansing, expulsion etc.
5. Statements characterized by a belief in their veracity, based on certain knowledge.

Oedipus at Colonos

1. No unambiguous answers (all is symbol; nothing is considered sign).
2. Smell, touch/feel, taste, emotion and quality as yardstick (+/− H, L).
3. Loneliness ("O"), darkness, i.e., no sense of sight to serve the purpose of orientation.
4. Community, connection, wholeness (+/− H; L; K; ♂♀; D).
5. Seeking, Enigma/Mystery ("O").

To my mind there is no doubt that the shift between the two figurations of Oedipus presents the psyche and its developmental potential. i.e., they indicate a psychotherapeutic space where actual development may take place. This happens by constant reconfiguration of the psychic states described in the two Oedipal myths.

c. A space for growth

Bion distinguishes between the *"Ding"* and the *"Ding-an-sich"*, where "things" are the reflections of moments between analyst and analysand, and the *"Dinge-an-sich"* are conditions in these meetings prior to the beginning of reflection. He terms these conditions "pre-conceptions" that meet and saturate "conceptions", and he uses diction characterized by images from physical reality, where coitus and breastfeeding are the most precise and descriptive conditions and metaphors for understanding any kind of meeting. Conversation is a process whereby we place words in each other's consciousness, just as the penis may be placed in the vagina during inter-course (also a synonym for conversation). When words are absorbed and seized, emotional consequences ensue and these may lead to creation, as when sperm meets egg. Clinical work serves to strengthen the possibility that meetings can be experienced, for meetings engender creation, creativity and life. When a meeting is unsuccessful and no saturation is achieved, the *"Dinge-an-sich"* arise, rather than concepts, thoughts or reflections, and the *"Dinge-an-sich"* become psychic junk or refuse (beta-elements). If the psyche is overloaded with junk it becomes what we may describe as diseased, characterized with excessive projective identification-conditions or different somatisations.

Psychic reality is phenomenological, meaning that it is prior to any form of verbalized, conceptualized, or perceptual thematisation. The essence of the psyche or consciousness is the current presence of the psyche vis-à-vis itself. Hence the psyche is at once emptiness and a capacity to contain. This capacity or suitability is defined or expressed through all present and possible accumulations of culture and knowledge. Thus consciousness is also that in principle unknowable limit of the possible. Hence the psyche becomes a sort of hyper-reflection. Maurice Merleau-Ponty does not say "cogito, ergo sum", but "sum, ergo cogito" (Langer, 1989, pp. 109–122). The notion that thought implies my being is fallacious: rather, the opposite is true. Through matter, form or body and neurological structure, thoughts are articulated both linguistically and non-linguistically. Thoughts are transformations of reality. The inner reality or prescience of consciousness becomes available as language, knowledge, theory and thought, through meetings where both realities relate plastically to one another.

In other words, every meeting between matter and form is creativity (Langer, 1989).

The mystery of conception would also seem to indicate this: sperm swarm around the ripe egg to an unknown choreography. The egg opens up as if responding to a hidden signal to a presumably chosen sperm and a new life can begin (Myskja, 2005).

This creativity-generating harmony at the cellular level might be of the same kind that arises between the psyche and "*Ding-an-Sich*" or the phenomena of the space of outer and inner reality. The body contains consciousness just as the uterus contains the foetus,

The growth we discussed in Section b. is growth in Euclidian space. We all know this space and this form of growth because we have grown accustomed to taking it for granted and because we have a psychic space (that we do not so easily take for granted) to hold it up against. We cannot form a physical space until we understand that we think and experience binocularly, i.e., through dualisms hence psychic space logically follows, since we do think binocularly or dualistically. Homer's texts are one illustration that this has not always been the case. His work does not include a Euclidian space separate from psychic space. Psychic space is—so to speak—non-existent and therefore physical space is perceived differently. Hence hallucinations or fantasies about the gods are imbued with a different status, becoming just as real as people and things. They are not formations of the psyche, which has yet to be thought. In Books 1 to 3 of the Odyssey, the description of Mentor's meeting with Telemachus concretizes young Telemachus' longing for his father's world in the figure of Mentor. Consciousness is unavailable as a space for immaterial objects; hence Telemachus' longing appears in concrete, rather than psychic form. Yet again Athene actively purveys this possibility by taking on the figure of Mentor as the space or consciousness of Telemachus. As Odysseus makes his way to the Phaecian capital after meeting Nausicaa, as described in Book 6, he is hidden by a cloud created by Athene. This illustrates that the notion of invisibility cannot be imagined since it requires a consciousness with- or without content. Consciousness has yet to be perceived as a space.

Athene intervenes to prevent Achilles from drawing his sword to slay Agamemnon, feeling violated because Agamemnon has robbed him of Briseis. Athene's action—the fact that she intervenes—becomes an expression of what we would now call "composure" (The Iliad, Book I, lines 190–251). Surely the act of "composing oneself" can be understood as a term for directing attention to the wounded, violated inner world and the emotions that will ensure. The Tantric science of consciousness formulates the same assumption, building its praxis on a systematic utilization of the emotional moment where attention strives to go beyond emotion, feeling, or the bodily—perhaps sexual—impulse. Tantric objectives are different to those in Homer's world or in usual situations of "composure", since it seeks to discover what lies behind emotion. Yet the techniques involved have the certain effect of reflecting action-impulses in a field that may be emotion-free, thus touching the creative force in which emotion rests and enabling a freer range of actions.

We encounter a similar situation in Homer's description of Achilles' meeting with his mother Thetis, to whom he laments (ibid, lines 350–425). He demands revenge for the humiliation he feels he has suffered since the lovely Briseis—his rightful spoil of war—has been taken from him. His psychic condition—the state of his inner space—is externalized in the events developed by his mother on the battlefield. The Greeks suffer defeat and the Trojans dominate the battle because Achilles is decisive in determining the balance of power. Achilles' wounded feelings are realized and his warrior's pride is vindicated. Psychic reality is communicated to the world through Thetis' divine intervention, but it is Thetis, not the psyche, that is perceived to be creating reality. The physical and the psychic worlds merge. There is no distinction between inner and outer objects, there are only objects (Zeruneith, 2002; Segal, 1988).

Phylogenetically and ontogenetically we have all thought in this archaic fashion and we are all still capable of doing so on occasion. Surely these are the modes of thought described by Hannah Segal's concept of "concrete thinking" and D.W. Winnicott's "transitional object". Bion believes that this archaic manner of thinking is related to psychotic thought and as such is distinct from neurotic thought. Psychoanalytic thought then, is a new, evolved mode of thought, characterized by being "O". Thus attention to physical space, psychic space—or an interplay of the two—arises from "O". Bion became aware of this state of consciousness, which he terms "O", through Klein's work on the primitive mental conditions she saw in children at the clinic, which she later found in the psychotic patients she was working with. Most people recognize these states—pre- and post-paranoid-schizoid conditions featuring narcissistic anger, or pre- and post-symbiotic conditions in cases like infatuation—where splitting, idealisation, projection and projective identification control consciousness.

I think "O" is what Sophocles is poetically indicating and describing in *Oedipus at Colonos*, as the place to which Oedipus goes when he disappears into the sacred grove. Merleau-Ponty speaks of how this extreme subjectivism is united with objectivity in Husserl's phenomenology. Therapeutic reality itself illustrates this paradox, since the therapeutic alliance allows both extreme subjectivity through the reciprocal presence of analyst and analysand and extreme objectivity through transference, which transform inner psychic reality into a mutual situation. This reality does not depend on interpretation; perhaps any interpretation is in fact the destruction of reality.

James S. Grotstein attempts to describe the spaces I have denoted as Euclidian and psychic space (Grotstein, 1990). He describes how Bion imagines a person staying in a three-dimensional world with representations of three-dimensional objects. Hence it becomes possible for him to match three-dimensional objects, which are projected into him from this world. These "hits" constitute his inner world, which he manipulates according to his current emotions or desires, both sleeping and waking. Thus we are dealing with two matching three-dimensional worlds, one outer and one inner, which can be freely manipulated through introjections/fantasies and projections/hallucinations—conscious as well as unconscious. Psychotic parts of people live in a different world, but it is via our attention to this fact that we can comprehend the nature of the neurotic world, just as we cannot understand darkness without light, love without hate, or good without evil. The neurotic world, however, is characterized by psychic objects such as beta-elements, alpha-elements, thoughts, pre-conceptions, which are subject to the rules of change—movement, transformation, etc.—that specifically apply to psychic space.

I am far from certain that I myself have completely understood these ideas and hence I shall try to describe them in several different ways. Most central concepts in Bion's thought appear to indicate, or even designate this understanding of space that I am trying to put together. First let me try to exemplify this thinking using an example from the clinic.

Bion characterizes the dyadic relationship between the concepts of container/contained or the Venus and Mars sign in alchemy which in Bions use means container-contained. He takes his cue from two universal sensory experiences, namely mouth-nipple and vagina-penis, turning them into metaphors of container-contained. In order to elucidate the tensile difference between the two qualities "contain" and "contained" he uses the alchemical sign for woman as a sign for contain, and the alchemical sign for man as a sign for contained. Bion emphasizes that these concepts should not be limited to metaphors of sex, body and gender, but seeks to define "mind" or consciousness in the broadest sense, where "mind" is a kind of "space-content space" encompassing space as well as content (Bion, 1970, pp. 71, 72–83 and 106–125). This idea can be schematized as follows:

Word as container

E.g. a word contains meaning as a meaning can contain a word, Bion exemplifies the latter by a person who stutters whenever he or she experiences emotional pressure to express an opinion or an emotion: that person is unable to express the word because the opinion or the emotional pressure contains it.

Words are sounded expressions and hence sounds or gesticulations in general can also contain a meaning that may be expressed and thereby contained through other media such as concepts, symbols, thoughts, and bodies. Consciousness is itself a container that holds everything while trying to find containers for this content, which may be identified or recognized as habits. The most primitive contents of consciousness are sensory data that are imbued with quality through the very fact of being contained.[6]

Memory as container

The metaphor container/contained is used to specify a significant difference between "recall" and "memory". Bion considers memory a container for something to be recalled.

We recall that which once was, while a memory is a re-experience, existing in the moment where memory is experienced in a session.

In Bion's words what is recalled "is in" or is contained in a temporal dimension while what is remembered "is in" or is contained in a sensory dimension. Hence memory is definitive for the "climate" of a session, corresponding to its sensory quality, while recall is an intellectual feat and as such peripheral to analytic work, however useful these feats of recall may be elsewhere (Bertelsen, 1999).[7] Another way of putting it is that memory establishes objective presence, in that absolute subjectivity becomes present to both the analyst and the analysand. Thus this phenomenon is created in a moment and this act allows change or development to take place, be it in the direction of D or Ps.

Dream as container

Dreams are significant because they contain emotion and attempt to free this emotion through their symbolic language. The fact that dreams are in themselves a verbalization means that they provide a certain degree of consistency and control over their emotional contents. Thus the dream becomes a container, whose symbolic language processes emotional material. The dream—or container—is active, dynamic and thus it is both a significant prerequisite to as well as a significant consequence of analytic work. The job of liberating that which is emotionally tied up in the dream and continuing to verbalize it is central to analysis because it creates memory, i.e., sensory *quality* in the sessions. Phenomenologically speaking this work recreates the world.

For this very reason dreaming is no different from thinking since the activity of consciousness is precisely about processing emotional material or sensory data, which are after all, qualitatively charged. Thought exists in consciousness and seeks a thinker, just as the dream exists in consciousness and seeks a dreamer. The thinker and the dreamer can then cooperate.

Similarly clients seek a therapist as human beings seek a fellow human being to be with.

Therapeutic space as container

Psychoanalytic activity is contained in time and space and within the framework that "contains" analytic activity. However, psychoanalysis cannot contain say, a client who does not show up or cannot stand to keep on showing up.

In the therapy-room, the laboratory or the alchemist's flask, call it what you will, the client can experience time and again that the articulation and staging of his or her own dyadic functions meet the analytic interventions of the therapist in the form of interpretation, empathy, acceptance or perhaps merely in the form of understanding, interest or attention. When the client brings anger, rejection or demeaning behaviour to the therapist, analytic intervention consists in *seeking* "truth" through words, symbols, and narrative, and if this is impossible then waiting, bearing frustration, tolerating it and letting it mature. Assuming this expectant attitude is an analytic intervention in its own right—particularly in relation to negative emotions, since it "contains" them without reacting.

In the following I shall provide a few brief examples from my clinical practice which cover the concepts outlined above.

The following material stems from T's third year of therapy.

> **T says:**
> A [A is T's 8-year-old son] had begun crying a little in connection with some of T and A's shared activities.
>
> T had told A that he wanted to spend time with A, but that it hadn't really worked out during the activities they had shared like tidying up, washing up, cleaning, etc. Then A had sat on T's lap for a while, sobbing and T had consoled him until A had lightened up and told him about a game he shared with his friends, that was real; that they had a power that they could use to communicate with each other. They could send real messages using this power and in so in a way it would touch one of the others and they would be connected to each other. They tried it with others and with some it worked and with some it didn't, but there were 4 of them where it worked well.[8]
>
> **I say:**
> Perhaps what A is describing is the way you are feeling yourself. So in a way you are sitting in my lap.
>
> Perhaps the power A is speaking of is the one he feels being with you on your lap and perhaps this is the same power that exists between us.

> During the following hour T tells me he has been thinking how important it is and has been for him to feel understood and to be met with tenderness and acceptance. During the next hour he suddenly remembers:
>
> That when he was two his father had taken him for a ride on his bike, which had a little seat on the crossbar in front and had taken him all the way around the lake. He felt a bit strange remembering this, since it must have been just him and his father all alone and his father must have done it for him.[9]

The memory of this significant togetherness between T and his father, where T is contained in his father's arms as they race around the lake is made possible by the fact that the feelings between T and me in the therapeutic space are experienced as allowed. The "containing" field thus encompasses A and T, T and T's father, as well as T and the therapist.[10]

It appears that the two examples here illustrate how therapeutic space or therapy can "hold" a client just as a memory can hold whatever emotion exists in the therapeutic space. The point is that the dynamic or emotion that exists between client and therapist is internalized and becomes an active object-relation to the client, who then takes a cue from this dynamic or emotion to constitute a number of other internal and external object-relations. The external object-relation is constituted between A and T while the internal one arises as a memory in T of T's childhood bike-ride with his father. Insight, memory and emotion are made possible through the therapist's interpretation; all this takes place in the psychic space that is created as it unfolds from Euclidian space.

At a significantly later stage the same client has the following dream:

> I am sitting in my car driving through some kind of town ... I'm driving. It's strange but I'm sitting in the wrong side of the car. I'm driving across a bridge and holding a very small child in my lap. He's just sitting there and we're having a really nice time.[11]

Although this dream is taken out of context there is no doubt that it expresses the fact that the dreamer is able to take care of his own needs for tenderness, as they appear to be expressed by the child he holds in his lap. He is able to give himself tenderness. The dream contains the desire, ability and need to take personal responsibility for one's inner child.[12]

Freud was of the conviction that we have sensory organs meant to perceive both internal and external stimuli. We are most accustomed to and practiced at using those relating to the outer world, but psychoanalytic sessions train us to use another, namely the organ that Freud himself trained during his self-analysis. Dream analysis and attempts to re-reflect dream traces during while awake are other ways of training this organ, as this clinical evidence seems to indicate.

This organ may also be strengthened through the training systems developed in the east through the "non-action" of meditation, a state surely reminiscent of the one Bion requires us to be in if we are to optimize our opportunities for growth; i.e., of neither memories nor desire, neither explanation nor expectation. Presumably, this was also what Freud discovered in his references to free-floating attention. Freud was aware of this state at a very early stage, since he describes it already in his 1893 eulogy for Charcot. Freud retells Charcot's demands to the doctor who *"faudrait y retourner et y rester"* [it is necessary to return and to stay there] when the doctors are with their patients at La Salpêtrière. He relates how Charcot demands that the incomprehensible must be observed over and over by the inner eye of consciousness in order for a sudden understanding to arise through the power of repetition. Charcot called this practical nosography and described a particular form of observation or non-activity, in which new things as old as the history of mankind were observed. It was not until May 25th, 1916, in a letter to Lou Andreas-Salomé, that Freud precisely describes the act of bringing oneself into a certain mental state, that may be characterized as the focusing of all light on a dark place. Alternatively he concentrates all attention on situations that appear to lack any form of sense or cohesion. It is well-known that Zen-training makes use of meaningless *koans* that may be similarly described as attempts to reaching higher, meaningful states and insights.

So it appears that the psyche is composed of mental processes that capture stimuli, consciously as well as unconsciously, from external and internal psychic objects through the senses. The psyche is our sense of thought, our thinking apparatus. These objects are differentiated by the desire or repulsion they give rise to. Bion establishes two types of stimuli.

One is the psychic type, which do not originate in the same three-dimensional world as the physical stimuli. There is an organ that captures these stimuli, and it is differently structured in the neurotic and psychotic parts of the psyche.

The second—entirely different form of stimuli—is the physical form, which we perceive in a manner similar to that of the many different kinds of apparatus we construct to measure temperature, sound, smell, taste, light, weight, shape, etc. It seems obvious, when there is a need for two such different entities—physical and psychic—that it must presumably be useful to place these entities in separate spaces. Only then do they achieve an ontological and epistemological position that makes it possible to approach them scientifically. Hence this shifting of the boundaries of metaphysics changes what can therefore meaningfully be discussed using scientific language, as these languages are or will be constructed.

Bion suggests that the transmitter of these psychic signals is broadcasting from "the void and formless infinite" as John Milton puts it, or from "O" in Bion's own terminology (Milton, 2007, p. 75, Book III, lines 12–13). But perhaps all signals, physical and psychic—are broadcast from the same shapeless void and are then perceived differently, depending on the way the receiver was adjusted by mother, father and other social and historical institutions in an onto- and phylogenetic perspective. This means that we perceive different realities, an idea which is not exactly revolutionary: babies and adults, tribal peoples and the inhabitants of industrialized societies live in the same, yet very different world.

The phenomenological world as discussed by Husserl is the common world, the one we are able to meet only subjectively with our psyches. This phenomenological world is also the only objective and true world. However, we do not share the "blueprints" we use to describe or command this only world that Bion terms "O", and which consists of phenomena. In this light it is understandable that we can actually communicate and understand one another and that we can work together to evolve towards greater freedom and truth. We do this with our subjectivity and thanks to common factors, both those that we seek and those we already possess.

Bion's project is to strengthen or train that sensory organ that perceives specific signals from this infinite, psychic abyss, this "O" which may be very different from the three-dimensional space of the outer world and its objects, but also has at least infinity in common with it and perhaps even begins and ends in the same place. One might say that there is a radio emitting signals (beta-elements, thoughts, pre-conceptions) from this space ("O") and a receiver—the psychic organ/consciousness—that must be developed and refined to improve reception of these signals and make it more precise and differentiated. On reception, the signals are processed, making them accessible to our consciousness using the alpha-function to transform them to alpha-elements for further processing. Our consciousness then turns them into myths, theories, scientific deductive systems, etc.,[13] in other words into humanity.

It appears as though these signals are the same as phenomena, perhaps the same as Plato's ideas and if the signals arrive as "lumps" or schemata, then perhaps also as the Jungian archetypes. However, we are in principle able only to momentarily access traces of these phenomena and/or their deduced shadows. We must accept that we see them as shadows on the dark back wall of a cave, to use Plato's example. Even a genius who has been outside the cave and beheld the light is blinded on his return and is unable to communicate his experience.

The languages we have developed serve to obtain skills in the form of control, power, possession, and security. However, the languages that we must develop to process signals from "the void and formless infinite" require an entirely different kind of processing, and serve only to hone attention. We must invent languages with which to listen. Bion suggests that this can happen by aiming "this beam of intense darkness" at all sensory impressions in order to turn off "memory and desire" as well as all passion and suffering, past or future. Understanding, cohesion, knowledge and insight, like a prohibitive, absorbent, underlying matrix of these "listening-states" must also be given up. Then this new articulation will take place, only to be given up once again.

It is thought-provoking that these recommendations are reminiscent of those given to Arjuna by the god Krishna before going into battle with/against his companions, to make Arjuna understand what kind of battle he is engaging in. Bion no doubt heard this story from his nanny and it is a literary poetic expression of the more theoretical guidelines proposed in Tibetan consciousness-training *dzogchen* as well as in Zen. Presumable we are dealing with a poetic description of the struggle to understand reality without doing so in a polarized or dual manner. Philosophically speaking, reality is considered monist, as a unity. In the monist view, dual or polarised description is false or at best, less true. Real understanding requires higher insight that is only achievable in certain states sought in mediation, whose objective is to reach a state of complete insight, or higher consciousness. It is asserted that in a way there is a kind of "mis-match" between the way our consciousness normally works and the world, so that our conception of the world, marked by our form of consciousness is "misrepresented". However, the mind or consciousness actually does have the opportunity to reach true insight through training.

This is the possibility expressed by Plato's cave-image as well as in many of his dialogues,[14] which the myths of original sin and the Tower of Babel of the Old Testament reject as impossible, and which Eastern training systems and the Gospel of Thomas in the Christian tradition claim is possible.

Psychoanalytic space is "binocularly" perceived. It involves two people who are not psychically separated but rather connected in transference/counter transference and whose communication is at once conscious and unconscious. The unconscious part consists of projections and identifications; the conscious part is the surface of what is being discussed. So there is a cognitive part where there is a certain agreement and clarity as to what is yours and what is mine, as well as an emotional part where the two merge. It is an open question whether the cognitive, dual part or the emotional unity is more real. This binocularity is clearly seen in transference, where the analyst is—ideally—attentive, i.e., directing his or her "gaze" at transference, while it is being discussed through or by that which took place in the past or may take place in the future. The analysand is attentive to his or her past/future, the analyst to the present, neurotically structured through transference and of which the analysand—again ideally and only if the timing is correct—becomes aware of when the analyst announces his interpretation of the transference, based on the material indicating the transference in the form of the contents of the conversation. Thus the analyst has binocular vision because he can keep his attention free of past and future, of feeling and cognition, at once asleep and awake and tied up in "O" where the structure of the psychic field between himself and the analysand then arises as an intuition. The analyst is "able" to perceive signals from "O". He may occasionally experience, as an expression of this ability, attacks on it in the form of intense, incomprehensible sleepiness overwhelming his mind during a session. This is a form of attack on the analyst's intuition, on his ability to think and maintain contact. I think these were the attacks Bion repeatedly referred to in his references to Vergil's story of Palinurus, who fell asleep at the helm one quiet night and was cast out to sea to drown still holding the rudder (Vergil, 1992–2000, Book V, lines 854–71).

> I also think that these conditions can arise, for instance, in couples' therapy:
>
> A couple who love one another have just had a child. The mother suffers post-natal depression and the father is promoted to a position in management. The child becomes ill and has trouble sleeping. After a year both parents are completely exhausted. The father suffers a nervous breakdown after a month of taking responsibility for the child at night to relieve the mother. They spend session after session blaming each other for their respective incompetencies and at home they boss each other around to demonstrate and demand a competent effort. Both are strongly aware of their own insufficiency and are angry at themselves and each other. Both feel powerless.
>
> At one point a certain relief is achieved when the therapist almost despairingly breaks the therapeutic framework by putting forward his own feelings of powerlessness at being unable to help, by not being able to solve the problems or make them go away.
>
> This understanding and compassion collectively holds the hopelessness of the situation in the therapist's suggestion following Paul to pray incessantly and give thanks in all conditions. This is an expression that goes back to previous sessions and reliefs of despair, maintaining that in the midst of all the misery, there is still much to be thankful for, because there is so much to learn.

Bion refers to this as the analyst's "reverie" or use of the alpha-function and is hereby expressing that the analyst has the same role vis-à-vis the analysand as a mother has vis-à-vis her baby. In this condition relevant thoughts can find their ready thinker, who must then be both analyst and analysand. What happens is that a series of repetitions are discovered during therapy, with identical sensory impressions appearing over and over; Bion's "constant conjunction" takes shape when repetitions "saturate" a concept which is then assembled into a distinct rhythm that eventually becomes a myth, a theory, a narrative. Thought, or the alpha-function, does the work, although we do not understand how this takes place. Similarly we cannot know what makes a song the kind of hit that attaches itself physically to the listener, like an inner sound.

Bion presumes that there are many different ways in which to express the intuitions of the "reverie", when the intense beam of darkness (the transmitter) is directed towards psychic reality (the receiver), transforming this darkness into different forms of symbolization. Off-hand we know of three whorls (vertices):

1. The scientific vortex, which we encounter when working with the "Grid" and other theoretical psychoanalytic work (before it achieves dogmatic status by being written down).
2. The religious vortex, which is expressed through acts of faith that create meaning, and activated through, e.g., interpretations, the use of theoretical systems, science or conceptualizations from couples-therapy *inter alia,* and hermeneutics. We encounter this when working in therapeutic space, in the dyad.
3. The aesthetic vortex as expressed and lived in music, art, poetry and literature. I shall attempt to exemplify this whorl in the section on symbolizations. Bion's *A Memoir of the Future* is an expression of this vortex.

d. Bion's epistemology and ontology

Bion formulated a reckoning with the part of Freud's thinking that was based on his biological, mechanistic reductionism, which again expresses the positivistic scientific ideals of the 1900s. Essentially this means that Bion associates Freud's theory of instinct with Plato's theory of ideas and Kant's *a priori* thinking. Bion calls Kant's *"Ding-an-sich"* or Plato's "ideas", "thoughts-without-thinker" or "pre-conceptions", which appear in the meditative state arising between analyst and analysand in the session. When they join to fruitfully let eruptions pour forth—free of memory and desire—stimulated by events in the inner or outer world in the now, they process these eruptions with the organ of consciousness. Thus this organ processes its matter, i.e., thoughts, just as the kidneys or the liver process bodily fluids, as the nose processes aromas and the eye processes light/darkness. So "thoughts" have existence like atoms, photons, and particles, but of a different kind and in their own space.

This understanding of ontology and insight articulates experiences described by Klein's concept of projective identification, which Bion understands not as simple fantasy, but as an expression of the analytical process itself and the changes (transformations) that take place through these processes of growth in which we are human, in- as well as outside the analytical dyad.[15] The experiences described by Klein are known in historical religious contexts, where they are described as common expressions of the psychic experiences of tribal people and of their view of nature and science. French anthropologist Lucien Lévy-Bruhl formulated the expression *participation mystique* to describe these phenomena (Lévy-Bruhl, 1926). Bion sees projective identification as a defence against attention to inner psychic processes. Projective identification thus becomes a more refined defence than acting out, in that it is not directly manipulated by external reality. Nevertheless projective identification is an action just like thinking.

Bion considers his idea an extension of Freud's thoughts on the two principles of psychic processes (primary- and secondary processes). Thus Bion describes the psychotic as primary processes, ensuring that psychic material is evacuated to avoid acknowledging disgust or a frustrating reality. Conversely the secondary processes modify disgust and reality through thought, i.e., by activating our thought apparatus, as it is constituted through interplay with the surroundings during childhood. The basic material here is the analytic dyad, and thereby thoughts. Thoughts are the atoms and molecules as they present themselves to the dyad. This is the stuff of psychoanalysis. The thoughts presenting themselves to the psychotic part of the personality are processed and shaped into psychotic thoughts, and the thoughts that present themselves to the neurotic part of the personality are transformed by it into the neurotic. A psychotic personality is unable to modify the thoughts with which it is presented and must therefore evacuate them, since the psychotic part of the personality is of a nature that is unable to make these thoughts the object of ordinary thought-processing. This evacuation can be conceptualised as projective identification and Bion terms the evacuated matter beta-elements, which are then experienced by the analyst as sensory data and emotions. Bion distinguishes between these impressions and the counter-transference of the analyst, perceiving counter-transference as a process that is always unconscious and can only be discovered through supervision or in-depth self-analysis, since counter-transference is the psychotic and neurotic side of the analyst himself; his own evacuations. Bion's insistence that the therapist has his or her own, unconscious, psychotic facets—and is therefore him- or herself connected with a formless black abyss—is significant, since this insistence is what maintains that therapeutic relations are more than asymmetric or unequal relations. In the dyad both participants are therapists and clients, and both are equally lonely, responsible and mortal.[16]

Through the evacuations of projective identification, the analyst becomes a container for these and must process them in order for the analysand to take them back in a modified form, through the interpretations provided by the analyst. It is during this work that the psychotic personalities of analysand and analyst are modified and become better able to process or merely discover thoughts that have become pre-conceptions. This development constitutes growth, increased freedom, and a rapprochement with truth. Naturally we may also speak of growth when neurotics discover their neurotic structure, even though it may be considered beneficial to continue acting these out, but in the choice between acting out and not doing so lies a form of freedom, as the Stoics said, freedom is the choice and acceptance of necessity.

This expansion of the concept of projective identification, which may be considered a container/contained function, can only be understood if we give up the subject-object dichotomy between analyst and analysand, and it is understood that analytic work takes place in a shared psychic space, where beta-elements are reshaped into alpha-elements. There is giving, receiving and giving back.

This analytic dyad creates an actual situation in which unbearable reality can be acknowledged as bearable, since the analyst demonstrates that this is so. Thus disgust or unbearable reality is modified and this modification can be learned through analytic experience. Evacuations then become less frequent or necessary, and excessive use of projective identification becomes increasingly superfluous. Psychotic defences are softened and the neurotic may become more sufficient.

According to this understanding, therapy actually heals through the activities that arise in consequence of the dyad constellating. Here we learn how the psychotic part of the personality, the primary processes, may be modified. These things are learned in the moment through the transferences that are formed when the psychic realities of the analytical dyad are discovered to be identical and modified. This frequently takes place through reconstructions of the past, present or future by working with dreams, fantasies or actions as they are expressed in the reality presented to the analytical dyad. Learning takes place when innate pre-conceptions meet realizations (in the analyst) in such a manner that concepts are formed. Bion requires no fantasies about an evil breast, some terrible combined object in a primal scene, nor an *uroboros*, although these concepts may be used as analogies for the container/contained situation or the Ps<=>D motion. The analytic process is the here and now being treated in that communication which is the dyad. During what is hopefully a creative symbiosis with the insane analysand, when the analyst her- or himself becomes insane and then well again—as has happened so often through the analysts own self-analysis and clinical experience—then a development takes place towards greater freedom, wholeness, trust and gratitude.

It is essential to understand that the work in this shared psychic space can only take place on condition that the separateness of the two individuals is recognized. We are not dealing with any kind of dissolution of identity in the dyadic symbiosis, but rather with a deep understanding of being oneself and being alone. The dyad must not be dissolved into unity, but rather precisely maintained as a mutually beneficial duality. When the analyst conceptualizes beta projection this takes place because the analyst becomes aware of aspects of his or her own psychotic personality. Then, if the ability to accept the ensuing interpretation is present, then both analyst and analysand learn.

Bion emphasizes the necessity for the analyst of liberating him- or herself of memory and desire,[17] entirely in keeping with Freud's emphasis on free-flowing attention and Klein's highlighting of projective identification as an attempt to fuse with the analyst in order to avoid feelings of chaos, which arise from the insurmountable demand to modify fantasies, internal situations of disgust or feelings of unbearable loneliness and separateness. However, Bion's theory on thought actually renders superfluous any assumptions as to these inner fantasies, since he merely speaks of beta- and alpha-elements. This entails the obvious advantage of allowing the analyst and the analysand to build up a systematic understanding of reality. In principle this work takes place using neither theory nor interpretation, since the moments unfolding during sessions form theories, concepts and understandings from scratch. The truth criterion is whether this work entails growth in the form of greater freedom and capacity for love. If successful, the analyst will avoid every form of acting out through thought and action on behalf of the analysand, and thereby also avoids participating in the assaults that will otherwise inevitably unfold through the transference-reactions of therapy.

Thus the really significant work takes place in the now, in the dyad between two separate individuals, unknown to each other, who have difficulties verbalising their separateness as well as thinking its forms, just as they find it difficult to meet and perhaps discover that their separateness was an illusion.[18]

I think that in spite of this separateness we are in one, single world; Bion takes a monist stand. The distinction between body and psyche are analytical tools and do not pertain to any reality other than the one set by the manner in which the human organ of thought is structured.

Writing in the early 1600s, John Donne (1570–1631) expressed this quite precisely in *"Progress of the Soul"*;

> ... her pure and eloquent blood
> Spoke in her cheeks, and so distinctly wrought,
> That one might almost say, her body thought.
>
> (Donne, 1994 [1612])

Hence to speak of an organ of thought is an approximation necessitated by the descriptive need for dualism and polarity; the organ of thought is the body and the body the organ of thought.

e. Transformations

Growth is defined by the change of something already extant, what Bion terms transformation. Nature holds magnificent examples of transformation: a tiny seed is placed in the ground and after 500 years it has grown into an oak of colossal dimensions. Dry, shrivelled, wrinkled chrysalides become beautifully coloured butterflies; tadpoles turn into frogs, etc., These transformations are all different to the type of growth sought in therapy. Nothing new arises, nothing is added or created. As previously mentioned, the object of all psychoanalytic endeavour is to create actual and thereby psychic change, contributing a psychic *novum,* thus rendering the process actually creative. In his theory of transformation, Bion attempts to describe psychic change, to deliver a theory and practice of psychic growth. This is also his agenda in the theory of thought he elaborated already in the 1960s, when his attempt to distinguish between psychotic and neurotic thought becomes a model of thought in general. In his *Cogitations* he remarks that Descartes, Leibniz and Newton all sought to formulate principles of psychic growth and that differential calculus was one such attempt (Bion, 1992, p. 320; see February 1971). Surely the Greek tragedians—at least in the cases of *Oedipus* and *Antigone*—as well as Plato through his entire philosophy sought the nucleus of creativity and growth?

In poetry, the brief pause marking the metre is called a cæsura. The entire rhythm is inherent in this pause; hence the actual quality or value of the verse arises from this gap. Similarly, change arises out of absolutely nothing. All we can do is describe the way towards the cæsura and onwards after it, but the growth of transformation takes place in the cæsura itself.

Michael Eigen makes an attempt to describe this cæsura, the point or beginning where change takes place, using the image of a dialogue where the parties have agreed to listen for what is unsaid behind each statement, trying to work out its meaning (Eigen, 1998). This means that nobody ever gets the final word; that top priority is given to listening for that which is unarticulated, and letting the conversation end with a question or an open silence. Such dialogue approaches "O". This performance is a sketch of what Merleau-Ponty calls phenomenological reduction or analysis, becoming a model of a kind of openness of speech to the unknown. Hence psychoanalytic activity becomes remarkably analogous to reflexive phenomenological analysis, rejecting the idea of a problem in understanding a fellow being or knowledge of the world, since it claims that we right from the birth of our consciousness have access to all forms of universal truth about ourselves and the other, who is of course identical to ourselves. Merleau-Ponty writes: "I am in no way distinguishable from an 'other' consciousness, since we are immediately in touch with the world and since the world is, by definition, unique, being the system in which all truths cohere" (Merleau-Ponty, 1962, p. 11).

Humanity has set itself the task of creating change through music and art. The painter reproduces landscapes, bodies or faces on a canvas; the sculptor transforms blocks of granite and marble. This is an attempt to achieve concurrence between their inner and outer worlds. The human body transforms and processes sensory impressions of touch, taste, sight and sound into products as diverse as food, music and mental images, but also into complex mental constructions and frameworks for action expressed into word, theories, laws, models, etc.

These transformations resemble those that take place when the lake reflects the sky. When the lake is turbulent the reflection is quite different to when it is calm, or to when a gentle breeze is blowing across its surface.

Different forms of change or transformation all involve one or more shifts between different whorls or "vertices". The concept of the "vertex" was coined by Bion and is to be understood almost as a point of view, a schema, or a paradigm of understanding. I prefer Bion's term because it focuses on the dynamically changing and involving element in any new horizon of understanding. Thus transformations are understood as a change of vertex. If we draw a line on a sheet of paper, the line itself—as well as the action of drawing it—exist in one vertex; we see the line as a mental representation in our inner world. This vision involves a change of vertex. It may change to a higher degree of mental abstraction through the arithmetic expression of a line x = ay without shifting, since this merely involves a different kind of mental abstraction. Vertex-shifts also take place when sound is transformed into signs c-d-e-f-g-a-h or are written as music. When sound is absorbed by our cells we may be carried away and we may cry, shiver or dance, thus expressing another vertex-shift. The singer singing the song that carries us away does not cry, shiver or dance, remaining instead in the vertex of the song or the sound although she is aware of the other (Myskja, 2005; Bion, 1984).

Play is another way of executing a transformation between inner and outer images; hence play is a transformation where an inner reality becomes external.

Perhaps psychotherapy is best understood as an attempt at rendering audible the theatre of the body. This theatre of the body is an expression of our motor skills, our cellular consciousness, our neurotic and hence unknown games vis-à-vis ourselves and each other. This is theatre that plays out tragically for prostitutes and drug addicts; it is also at work in power-seeking and successful politicians and businessmen. We are bound by un-freedom in our escape from the unbearable in the form of separation, betrayal, assault, and disrespectful, intrusive behaviours. Our day-to-day living expresses a lifelong reckoning with—at best—good-enough parents. It seems that we cannot or will not settle for good-enough in our striving for goodness, or perhaps these reckonings are simply what we call life.

Even before children start speaking, this reckoning or "life" begins in their interaction with the surroundings expressed through play, sound and movement. Through the way they behave, children are telling and creating stories. Their expressions become interpretations, transformations of the reality they are co-creating through their behaviour.

Below I have given an example of this play-transformation as seen through the eyes of an adult observer. Here the observer attempts to describe the dynamic interaction between child, mother and father.[19] The following is an excerpt of an observation-report. The baby is about one year old and at this time the mother has just returned to work after spending a year on leave caring for her child at home. At the time of observation, it is the father's turn to pick up the child from day-care and spend time with him at home. The observer arrives:

> *Tuesday February 14, 1995 at 16.00.* The father is standing in the hall with Kim by his side waiting for me as I enter. At first Kim glances at me with a rather empty expression, then a bit surprised. He gives me a hesitant smile that broadens into a full-faced grin. I say hello a couple of times. Then I touch his head in a friendly manner and say hello again. He turns and points at the rack where I usually hang my coat and I do what he seems to want me to do. He runs ahead into the bedroom and throws himself head-first onto his parents' bed, bending his head and chest down to the mattress. I imagine a primal scene.

It has become a little easier for Kim to recognize me at this stage. He has learned to deal with this new situation, and seems to be participating in the session from the outset, identifying with his mother: ordering me to place my coat on the hanger, showing me who is in charge and pointing out that he knows what is going on in his parents' bed.

> He then takes a toy, some sort of tin, in the corner of the room. He slams it onto the bed and then throws it on the floor. This makes quite a noise and he repeats it a number of times. His father does not mind. I find it too noisy. Kim seems very happy. He emits loud little screams of joy and runs to the long curtains in the bedroom. He plays with them, embracing them. He runs into the sitting room once again heading for the curtains. His father says that he is playing "catch" but does not try to catch him. Kim keeps looking over his shoulder to see if I am following him as he runs into the dining room, where he runs over to a chair and bends his upper body to lie across it, half sitting half standing.

In this part of the session Kim is repeating a game he often plays with his mother. She would chase him around as he hid in the curtains, now he himself is doing the chasing. He shows me this game, realizing that I must know what is going on. He is using me as a mirror, through which to identify with his mother. He is overcoming the loss he has suffered through separation by using me to identify with, as some amalgam of mother and observer.

> Next he runs over to a glass-fronted bookcase. He stands in front of it for a very long time, trying to reach the books, leaving sticky fingerprints on the glass. His father says that he believes that I was right in my remarks the other day, that he is showing me what new things he has explored since the last time I was there. I say I have never seen him like this before. He sometimes screams with joy, and makes all sorts of other sounds as he runs around the flat.

I guess that his joy indicates that he feels very safe identifying with his mother. Nevertheless the identification is a manic defence which is tolerated by his father and facilitated by my presence, which leads Kim to remember that I used to come and be with him and his mother. I believe that the father needs this manic defence, which is a more sparkling, positive front than all the negative emotion related to loss and separation. Yet the strong manic defence indicates a corresponding strength of negative emotion. Kim may be afraid of falling apart, grieving for the loss of his mother, while his father is afraid that he will not be able to manage Kim's fear. Thus Kim's defence mechanism is perhaps just as much a protection of his father as of himself, and he feels assisted in this by my presence.

> He runs from the bookcase to the glass door separating the dining room from the study, a room his father says he is not normally allowed to enter. Nevertheless Kim insists on having the door opened. After a while his father gives in. Kim runs into the room and heads straight for a set of sand-pit toys stored in there. His father proudly says that Kim must have remembered that the playthings were in there and was able to insist on getting them. He seems a little insecure as to whether pride is the correct emotion and adds that Kim might just have seen the toys as he entered. I believe he might have remembered that they were in there. He takes the bucket and sits on the floor, beginning to play with the set. His father tries to get him to move into the sitting room by telling him that it is too cold in the study, which seems unheated. After a while his father stands Kim up, takes

> hold of his hand and walks him into the sitting room, where he sits on the floor with him and continues to play with the bucket. I get a glimpse of a fantasy that this brings him closer to his mother, but it seems a bit unfair. The father tells me that he picked Kim up early because they rang from the crèche to say that he was unwell. We agree that he does not seem too bad, but of course he does have a cold. I say he was probably pining for his Daddy. We agree on that. Kim plays for a while with the bucket, accidentally putting it on his head like a hat. He looks very funny and smiles, either feeling that he is somehow pleasing us or enjoying the strange feeling of the bucket on his head. His father decides to take a picture. He fetches the camera, but now Kim wants it and refuses to put the bucket on his head again. His father gives up on the photograph, saying that now Kim will be angry because he is replacing the camera on top of a bookcase. Kim does indeed get cross, screaming his protest and beginning to cry. I think of Fordham's concept of deintegration[20] although Kim soon forgets the camera as his father caresses him. He runs over to his teddy bear and lies down on it; rises quickly and runs back to the curtains to play with them, falling a few times. Then he gets up, runs over to a truck to play with it. I fetch coffee, and Kim has a cup of juice.

The important thing is Kim's sense of being in charge: entering the forbidden room; handling the toys; making himself the centre of attention by putting the bucket on his head; being photographed. As soon as he loses the feeling of being in control, when his father decides against taking the photograph, he seems to disintegrate. Then he manages to take hold of himself by cuddling his teddy bear rather than being cuddled by his father, since cuddling the bear and playing with the curtains makes him feel like his mother. He re-establishes his identification with her. I think I can interpret my fantasy about his mother as a projective identification in which Kim signifies his unconscious feelings of missing her. His father, however, also identifies with the mother, making things run as smoothly as possible and taking charge of both Kim's needs and mine:

> Suddenly the kitchen door opens and I hear Kim's mother entering. His father says from the sitting room: "You're home

> early". I am glad to have this opportunity to see both parents with Kim. At first, Kim becomes serious, then smiles, and when his mother enters the room—after watching her for a while—he turns his back on her and takes a few steps away, then he turns again and runs to her for a hug; he runs back to the curtains and she runs after him hugging him again. They repeat this several times laughing and giving loud shouts of joy. Kim's father gets a hug and so do I.

The question here is what to do when reality exposes you: Your lost mother is suddenly present, revealing your identification as false. No wonder Kim feels insecure and uncertain as to what to do. He soon manages to get himself together, however, mostly using his curtain-game and—judging by the high spirits—the joy seems not to be manic defensive. Later in the session Kim identifies with his mother in a number of ways: he takes a sponge from the bathroom, and touches all the buttons on the washing machine. Amongst other things this makes it possible for her to talk to me while he is busy playing either by himself or with his father.

> (Kim plays alone or with his father, while I talk to his mother) Time is up. I must relax from my intense attentive state. I take another cup of coffee, chatting a little to Kim's mother. After a while she says she is very tired. We finish our talk about her new life, coming home tired, etc. About twenty minutes after her arrival I say that I need to leave. Kim's mother says that she needs a nap. I wave to Kim and get up. I wave again. Kim runs ahead of me into the hall to the door. I follow him. I put on my coat. Kim is waiting in front of the door. He waves. I wave. I open the door and wave, saying goodbye to his parents and telling them that I will see them next Tuesday. I close the door. I hear Kim crying behind the door. I feel sad and angry; there is a sudden pain in my chest. I am thrown into my own fear of separation and tears well into my eyes. This happens again as I write my notes from the session early the next day. I have to take a long break to soothe myself. I wonder why I did not write my notes yesterday, unconsciously wanting to avoid the depression by being fully with my own son. I feel depressed.

The last part of this section reveals the strength of the projections and how the child's unconscious melds with that of the observer. The extreme joy that follows Kim's hesitant welcome of his mother is a cover for the severe difficulty he has admitting his grief at the loss of his mother. I believe these are also the feelings of his mother, based on her own description of her feelings at having to leave Kim in the morning before he wakes up and not seeing him again until late in the afternoon, as well as her fatigue after our talk. The strong bond between Kim and his mother is evident in his ability to play alone or with his father in order to give his mother a chance to deal with her pain by talking to me. We try to prepare for the blow of separation by the repeated waving, but the more we wave, the less we succeed. Kim weeps and I feel a sudden pain in my heart or chest. My anxiety is aroused, finding bodily expression and forcing me to reflect on my own loss and fear of separation. The power of these emotions may be seen from the fact that they actually make me postpone my usual routine and even last into the following day.

> During the following period Kim was unwell. He suffered from a cold that made life very uncomfortable for him. He lost a considerable amount of weight, had no appetite and was weepy and difficult to comfort. Our sessions were full of pain and sorrow. For two weeks I was unable to take notes after these sessions and felt inclined to give up.

The following conversation, which took place during a therapeutic session, is another expression of this anxiety that may seize a person faced with a real—i.e., an existential life-change. At this point the client was in his 3rd year of therapy and there had been much talk of the ability to open up and trust. During the previous session X had announced that he could not deal with a woman who refused to be penetrated. The theme then becomes one of power and control vis-à-vis surrender not only during sex but in other day-to-day activities. X is annoyed that his wife will not surrender to him, that she cannot open up. He feels betrayed, lonely and rejected:

> In the following, X relates that his wife's Christmas cookies have disappeared. Someone stole them and ate them, perhaps the children, perhaps the au-pair. I think of the metaphor of being "caught

> with your hand in the cookie-jar", of robbery and surreptitious appropriation. However, I also think of the shame and the anxiety of not being able to express ones desires and the grief when they cannot be satisfied. X tells me how, a few days previously, he had told his wife of his longing, of how he felt betrayed and rejected. He had really tried to keep the ball in his court, expressing that he was taking responsibility for his own feeling, but that this was the way he felt. He was suffering and could not bear it. At this point the conversation developed into a vicious argument. He reported that his wife had been very angry and had told him that he was waiting for her like a demanding child when she came home, that she could not tolerate his childish greed. The argument ended with X going out on the town. The next day he had not felt hung over so much as sick of himself ... a moral hangover, so to speak. He felt he had given in, like in the old days; he was sick and tired of the repetition. However, the day passed normally. When he got home he sat down in his usual chair to relax for a while. He heard the door open and his wife entered. She resolutely went straight over to him, got on her knees in front of him and apologized. This had never happened like that before, X said.

During the following conversation we discuss how she in a way penetrates him through her resolve and directness, her openness and surrendered body language on her knees between his legs. I say: "It is as if she is surrounding you with her open mind, her open arms, her open vagina and entering you between your legs. Everything is open and you are at once brought in and invited in".

The atmosphere in the therapy room is soft and silent. I have series of images of receiving a kneeling woman in embracing forgiveness between my open legs in a chair as well as images of coitus, where I am the female part, opening up to receive my partner in a kind of soft, embracing bliss.

I ask X: "How did you feel with her in the chair in front of you?"

X says that he had been expecting to be scolded for going out. After a small break he says: "I got a fright. I've never experienced it before; I think it was anxiety, but only for a split second".

I say: "She showed you trust".

X pulls a face and turns his side to me, squeezing his legs together and pushing forwards his right shoulder and says: "That anxiety made me turn away from her".

I feel deeply touched by the situation and say: "It is really difficult for you and for her to trust and accept that you are not always sufficient for each other. But there she is, coming to you with her trust and strength, asking you to accept it. She wants to put that acceptance into you and you give her the cold shoulder. Perhaps you also have difficulty opening up when she wants to—so to speak—enter you".

X says: "I can see that in a way I perhaps do not let myself be penetrated".

I say: "In a way it is strange: at the moment when you realized that she had actually shown you her trust earlier, when I interpreted her body language for you, you repeated your rejecting body language. In a way you let your body reject my interpretation, like you rejected her, and yet it is as if you understand that this is what you are doing".

We speak of how frightening it can be for a man to give up his role as the penetrator, his entire self-understanding—and for him to discover that he has the ability to hold; if not physically through his sex, then at least metaphysically through his attitude and consciousness. It seems to be a threat to identity and means giving up your masculinity, being eaten up by your mother. But perhaps the courage and ability to do this are an aspect of masculinity, just as they are an aspect of femininity.

We go on to discuss the anxiety that kicks in when we discover that we can change something in ourselves, when we are able to see it; the anxiety and fear of being overwhelmed, swallowed up, annihilated by the goodness of life" (Meltzer, 1988).

In my opinion there are several principally different forms of transformation at work in the two family situations listed above as experienced by me through the baby-observation and the therapy session: Different forms of growth are being resisted with various forms of defences and with varying degrees of success.

If the situations as they were are termed "O" then all linguistic formulations, interpretations or theories are a movement away from "O". They become transformations or disfigurings or a kind of destructive attack on "O". These are carried out by a person whose structure is the disfiguring lens through which "O" is seen. However the structure or "lens" of this person is altered through interpretation, but "O" is also altered since "O" is part of both the personalities involved in the situations. Thus the meetings or situations create growth that may be acknowledged by the people involved, although this is not necessarily the case.

The people involved may realize that change has taken place, which is precisely what happens in the situations referred to here. The strange thing is that while growth appears to take place in "O", is distortedly perceived through interpretation, and then taken up "truly" in "O", which is once again distortedly interpreted but this time in a new manner. The difference between these interpretations gives cause to reflect on their nature. What direction was chosen Ps<=>D? Are we moving from exclusivity and polarity (Ps) towards and acceptance of complexity, greater inclusion and unity (D)? Is more hate or more love being expressed? Or are we dealing with the opposite direction and hence "misguided growth"?

All change or transformation implies disgust, hence neurotic and psychotic personality-aspects are used to fight it, as Freud showed in his theory on defence. I shall attempt to describe this Sisyphean psychic labour in Chapter Four.

The way growth is fought or accepted gives rise to the names of the various forms of interpretations or transformations. Through minute description, Bion hoped to make it easier to achieve freedom. He outlines five typical forms of transformation: hallucinatory, identificatory or projective, transformations in "K", catastrophic transformations, and transformations in "O" (Bion, 1984, pp. 36 and 42 ff.).

1. Hallucinatory transformations

While these transformations are used especially by people with a paranoid structure, we all have access to them and do utilize them to various extents. However, insight into paranoid defence stems chiefly from people with schizophreniform symptoms, where hallucinatory transformations are particularly evident.

Bion (1993) describes how a patient who has been diagnosed with schizophrenia takes "parts" of Bion in via the eyes, only to project them directly into a corner of the consultation space in a less dangerous or non-intrusive form, located in a place where they may be kept under control (Bion, 1993).

Bion claims that "these parts" are haunting aspects of the patient's own psyche, which were disposed of through projection in an earlier session (Bion, 1984). This mechanism may be understood from a notion that sensory organs may be considered to have both projective and introjective ways of functioning. Paranoid personality aspects make particularly frequent use of these functions, often in a very violent manner.[21]

These functions take on a more discreet role only when the psyche has obtained considerable maturity as well as a capacity for abstraction, thus allowing social interaction to run a more nuanced course, where the sensory and emotional components of the psyche are positioned extra-psychically. Thus the client no longer perceives everything as "me", since a comprehension of an inner and an outer world has been formed (Bick, 1988a & b; Fordham, 1976). The fact that anyone may relapse into a previous mode of functioning is particularly evident in group analysis and in couples therapy, where the parties and participants often have difficulty holding onto their own emotions, and it often becomes necessary to remind oneself and others to play the ball from their own court and to show respect and caution when in the territory of others.

Hallucinations may ensue when one's own emotions become unbearable and the psyche of the other is perceived as haunting. In cases of pathological jealousy the other is perceived as unfaithful, unloving or rejecting in lieu of addressing one's own feelings of insecurity and low self-esteem. The other is hallucinatorily seen as false, loose, and cold, thus displacing or projecting one's own memories of loss, greed, failure to love, and betrayal.

Thus hallucinatory defence appears as a distortion of outer reality when the inner world can no longer be contained. Affective personality types also make defensive use of hallucinatory transformations. The depressed client experiences attacks on his or her own inner world, where feelings like worthlessness, defeatism, disgust and loss of meaning, change perceptions both of the self and of the outer world. The manic position involves a different form of distortion, but one that is at least as distressing to the surroundings.

The only way to create psychic growth towards greater freedom and truth is through a softening of these defences.

2. Identificatory or projective transformations

One of the decisive difficulties in discussing psychic growth lies in the fact that the psyche is a "non-object". We cannot create direct contact to the psyche using our senses or the instruments we know of to extend and sharpen them. Anxiety and love cannot be sensed or measured.[22] Thus the sciences of the psyche are distinct from other sciences, particularly natural sciences, whose theories and models are closely linked to the notion of the existence of objects in a space that contains them. Theories of natural science are object-realizations.

Psychological theories are realizations of "non-objects". Hence a theory of psychic growth is a theory of changeable "non-objects".

The hallucinatory transformation mentioned above is an attempt to dispose of unwanted psychic entities or "non-objects" by turning them into "objects". Anxiety is projected by turning it into something frightening and external to the psyche. Everyone knows the waking nightmare of children, where a jacket on a chair becomes a dangerous ogre. Many of us have banished our childhood fears under the nursery bed transmogrified into trolls or monsters, leaving us too terrified to get out of bed. Thus our nameless anxiety is transformed into things in the outside world for the psyche to identify with.

Many adults discover that they may be seized by negative emotions, distorting their vision of their surroundings and the people to whom they are attached. They may see their husband, wife or lover as cold, angry, ugly, fat, hairy, disgusting and self-absorbed, or sometimes the opposite. These perceptions can change in the course of a single day. The psyche is attempting to dispose of the matter that is overloading it. That with which it cannot deal itself must be transferred to others. One's own emotions become object-relations associated with other people.

Somatisation is a particular form of projection; here feelings or personality structures are projected from being "non-objects" in psychic space to being "objects" in the body, where they may settle as poor motor skills, stiffness, infiltrations, or as outright somatic disease. Presumably the body reacts at a micro- or cellular level to far more stimuli than we are currently aware of.

Every relationship involving people holds similar identificatory processes. Psychic space is not delimited by the same rooms as objective space. The psychic space of an individual is not delimited in relation to other individuals but is a common space. Hence psychic content can move freely, allowing individuals to understand and empathize with one another.

One of a baby's first actions is to try to swallow the nipple that appears, and which the baby desires. It has not yet learned the difference between objects and "non-objects", me and you, inner and outer, and past-present-future, etc., Later people may gorge and gag on objects, money, knowledge, etc., thus creating links with their surroundings as well as with other people. Biomass, knowledge, habits, and behaviours are individual, more-or-less processed identifications of the surroundings. Internal object-relations express external ones which the individual has internalized and identified with. The patterns created constitute a constantly growing organism that we may attempt to structure using concepts, theories or schematizations like ego, self, superego, complexes, archetypes, neuroses, psychoses, etc., Psychic mechanisms, however—including projective transformations from the very beginning of life—are always available. Everybody uses them and many diseases are an expression of the fact that we frequently do so inappropriately.

Biological mechanisms may be a metaphor for psychic processes. It makes good sense to describe the psyche as a digestive system; building large elaborate psychic constructs from the matter it takes in and rejecting that which is superfluous. However, that which it is unable to reject becomes encapsulated. In other words psychic metabolism is transformation as is the physical.

Many of these mechanisms prevent growth, others promote it. They all ensure psychic stability through the elimination of undesired psychic components. The psyche both desires and rejects growth. People engage in lifelong battles for and against growing up and maturing, which persist through all our sleeping and waking hours (Grinberg, 1990; Meltzer, 1970 & 1986).

3. Transformations with "K"[23]

These transformations are generally considered to be the forerunners of growth, but since there is a distinction between "knowledge of" and "being", forerunners they remain. The work of obtaining "knowledge of" can hence be used to oppose growth, where growth is once again understood as real change which allows the changed individual to be present in a new mode of being. The individual "is" in a new way. This is a somewhat clumsy formulation and hence Bion speaks simply of changes in and with "O". Thus he is trying to express that growth is a movement that has taken place or is taking place into something unknown that cannot be described, since that which is described must naturally somehow be known to some extent. Hence descriptions of growth are an expression of something that—at best—*was* growth (López-Corvo, 2005; Bion, 1984).

The reason "knowledge" tends to oppose growth is that it is often mistaken for growth. Knowledge is the result of growth, but is at the same time different from growth. In therapy the battle against growth is particularly evident in intellectual defence and intellectual "acting out". This may happen when a client intellectually accepts an interpretation, but does not wish to take on the emotional or active consequences of this interpretation. Of course it may also be seen in situations where the therapist has fallen upon a true guess, but where the client is using his energy and resources to intellectually reject this interpretation. "True" guesses at the wrong time are no good. It can be extremely difficult to distinguish the different forms of defence. Yet the significance of doing so may be exaggerated since the growth to which we aspire takes place in "O" and not through mental or intellectual manipulations engaged in by the therapeutic couple in the course of therapy. Perhaps this is why true change is always discovered with a great sense of wonder some time after it has actually taken place, giving rise to awe and gratitude. This sense of wonder can then form the stepping stone to new forms of insight and perhaps to further growth.

As long as "K" transformations are perceived as being processual they indicate a way through development to growth. Accumulating knowledge does not become a goal in its own right, but rather a kind of running start. Knowledge becomes a kind of diving board for the leap into the deep unknown, the mighty space in which actual growth may take place. When this is experienced it becomes a kind of catastrophic condition. One of the advantages of therapy is that such catastrophic conditions can be prepared by and shared with a therapist, who hopefully has the calm and experience to deal with catastrophic psychic conditions, trusting that they—like most stormy conditions—shall pass. Perhaps the prerequisite for this is the reasonably calm space ensured by a stable, therapeutically internalized object-relation, consisting of the analyst and the analysand in a commensal or good-enough working relationship.

During the attachment phase people live through a series of traumatic events. Classic psychoanalytic theory agrees that birth is decisive; similarly the meeting with the breast and later the weaning process are seen as traumatic events. People are made for and learn from these traumas. Some children, however, experience an inner catastrophe in relation to stronger, more enduring and repetitive traumas with which their caretakers fail to deal in a sufficiently communicative fashion. I think that the observation detailed above shows the processing of such a trauma. The tremendous sadness and the child's ensuing somatisation infects the observer, who becomes depressive. The situation is linked to his own traumas and experiences of broken threads in the fabric of the soul. This very experience however, contributes to the healing of such broken threads. The sadness is felt and attended to.[24] The process of creating the confidential relationship between the therapist and the client through a solid and sufficient inner representation becomes immensely significant. Still, threads may break too frequently and violently, resulting in psychic illness. Thus in serious cases a stricken person cannot bond with anyone, not even a therapist. It becomes impossible to forge a stable framework to constitute a common psychic space between therapist and analysand. The framework is destroyed, therapists are replaced one after the other and the threads break over and over.

Therapy is long-term treatment whose success depends not only on the capability of the therapist but on the maintenance of regularity and frequency throughout the course of therapy.

There is one particular transformational form among the "K" transformations, which Bion terms "rigid-motion transformation" (Bion, 1984, pp. 18–19). He emphasizes the importance of distinguishing these from projective mechanisms, finally comparing them to transferential neuroses, whose creation and dissolution may be one of the means to ensure growth in "O". These transformations are connected to the external framework of therapy. They ensure the optimal trust that is prerequisite to overcoming the anxiety provoked by growth.

When the therapist discovers that situations in the clinic are a kind of repetition of certain behavioural patterns played out by the client in his or her daily life, the therapist may successfully suggest interpretations of the interaction between them, in the hope that the client will recognize that this is going on. Frequently, changes in the interaction occasion such discoveries. For instance, the therapist may be occupied with something when the client rings the doorbell and it may take an unusually long time before the client is buzzed in; or therapy may be interrupted by the postman at the door with recommended letter, forcing the therapist to open the door. The anxiety arising in such situations may be used to indicate the significance of external frameworks overall and may thereby lead to a discovery of the role of anxiety in other settings and not least of the distorting significance of anxiety on the perception of these connections. Perhaps—although this is of minor significance—the anxiety can then be traced back to traumatic situations in the client's life, when and if these appear in memory. Growth does not arise through the repetition of such events, but because the ability to tolerate frustration and anxiety is strengthened through the minor shocks that arise when a stable, therapeutic situation is exposed to the changes inevitably created by life; here produced in a manageable fashion during therapy.

Counter-transference phenomena are also an expression of this type of transformation in that they create a connection between the unconscious feelings and emotions when the therapist discovers feelings and emotions in him- or herself, which he/she assumes have arisen through the relations laid out in the ongoing communication between him- or herself and the client (Grinberg, 1990). Most people are familiar with the feeling of being moved by the suffering of others, or being happy for them. We speak of an infectious laugh or joy, and we cry when those we love grieve. The therapist may be attentive to similar reactions, using them to intellectualize or interpret the interactions they express, through so-called transference interpretations. Clearly only the parts of intra-psychic communication that relate to the client are of interest here. Thus the therapist must only acknowledge his familiarity with these kinds of emotions by referring to them. The therapist must be able to bear withholding his own emotions. Thus transformations in "K" are facilitated, since the client becomes familiar with aspects of his or her emotional life that previously were less familiar, while having the opportunity to experience sharing these personality aspects with another.

Such counter-transference transformations must be distinguished from situations, where the therapist does not discover that the client has transformed aspects of the therapist, i.e., that the therapist's subconscious has been altered or transformed. These transformations belong in the category of projective identifications and are what León Grinberg terms projective counter-identifications. They are caused by a lack in self-knowledge on the part of the therapist and may give rise to various forms of acting out. Like all exaggerated projective identifications they are counterproductive, since they block insight and are a burden on the therapeutic relationship. Sexual transferences are among the most debated of these conditions and it is generally acknowledged that any form of acting out is inappropriate in such cases (Grinberg, 1990).

4. Catastrophic transformations

I think Bion's concept of "catastrophic change" may be used to elucidate actual growth and the creation of the really new.

He describes catastrophic change as a psychotic breakdown that runs through different phases (Bion 1984, pp. 6–11). However, he describes it from the outside, so to speak, by describing a series of psychic, somatic and behavioural conditions that may arise in the patient, the therapist and those who surround them (Searles 1979). These events may be compared to an explosion and there are three stages: 1. Explosive material is gathered or created; 2. The explosion, and 3. The blast wave. These events are played out under controlled circumstances during therapy and may here be divided into an initial phase, where the client does not appear to change vis-à-vis the therapist or his surroundings. This has the appearance of a denial pattern. There seem to be no violent emotional disturbances in the therapeutic relation and any "violence" is predominantly of an intellectual nature, although the client experiences it as a severe threat to his or her surroundings. There are also extensive projective identifications.

During the following central phase, catastrophic change takes place at a point in a space of consciousness, whence it spreads and creates consequences for the surroundings.

In the following I shall try to show how this central phase may play out, using the interplay between myself and X. The change takes place in our conscious space, spreading out from there like rings in the water:

> X tells me that his sexual fantasies are almost always about satisfying a woman and experiencing her desire, that this is what legitimizes his own desire. X says he finds it very difficult, that it is like having to live your life through others. He feels he can only exist through others.
>
> I say that then he feels as though he himself is dead unless he can borrow the desire of another. Yet what you are doing is fantasizing that others have a desire that makes it impossible to reach out to them, since you run the risk of discovering that they have no desire except in your imagination, but then in a way you discover that you yourself are dead, are nothing.
>
> Perhaps you feel that by reaching out your hand and putting it on her shoulder, to draw her to you, you risk discovering that you yourself are dead. Or you discover a kind of dead spot inside spreading and perhaps killing her too.
>
> Then there is nothing.
>
> X stands up to leave, then sits down again. He says: you got it exactly right and I want to leave, because I can't bear it.
>
> **I say:** You feel as though you have been dropped. You are seeing stars, or whatever the term is for that experience just prior to fainting. Have you ever fallen and hit your head and fainted and do you remember what it feels like?
>
> X says that he fell once when he got up in the night to urinate when he was very tired. He fainted and hurt himself and had to go to the casualty ward for stitches. As he went down he had the experience of everything disappearing, of dying and dropping his life on the floor.
>
> **X continues:** I am terribly afraid that I will turn out to be mad, that the black hole will swallow me up and that I'll find out that that's all there is.
>
> X tells me of his mother and her untreated post-natal depression followed by treatment for depression after the birth of her third child. The mother was lonely after moving to xx, she had no friends while she was pregnant and tried to abort

> X and wished him gone when he was born and when he was inside her.
>
> X says that in a way she dropped him and now he feels as though she was a fish when he thinks of touching her: it is cold and if he squeezes it then it will disintegrate into some black nothingness.

In consequence of this discharge or controlled psychotic breakdown (Bion, 1984, p. 7), X is able to remember his emotions, rather than simply remembering what happened.

At the same time I attempt to associate his memory to earlier transference experiences in relation to me:

I say: do you remember the themes we discussed in your first year here? X asks me to sum up and I briefly tell him how he kept saying he could not trust me, and if he did he thought I would immediately discontinue therapy or somehow turn out to be rejecting or critical. He was afraid to believe that I wanted or was able to cope, or to believe that he himself wanted to or could.

X agrees.

Then I say: what you were afraid of was that if you trusted me, you would discover that I was not there, that I was dead. If you reached out for me and touched me you would yourself feel cold and death.[25]

That night I have a nightmare. My psyche becomes a sounding space for the collapse that took place during the session as the blast wave expands across it.

I dream:

> An infinite black hole with a kind of crystalline latticework of even blacker bars. I am that hole and when I "wake" from the nightmare I feel that I keep on being the hole. It has no body, just matter in bars and blackness. It is almost impossible to emerge from. I turn, wakefully (still dreaming) trying to feel my wife, but she is gone, or else I just cannot reach her. It happens over and over. I wake up a little more and look at the clock, it is 3 a.m. I grow a little calmer and understand that it is a nightmare.

> I cannot get out of bed, since I have no orientation. All is black matter and I am seized by a powerful anxiety in the form of stiffness and heaviness if I try to move even a little. I fall back into the nightmare, dreaming this time that I see Oedipus walking into the grove by the alter to that unknown place where he disappears into darkness and death.

The dream coupled with X's feeling of the proximity of death and X's flight-response are all signs of a change making itself increasingly felt. One measure of the depth and effect of these changes is the impact on my unconscious through my nightmare. The effect continues in the work subsequently carried out in therapy, where I use my dream as a starting point for the interpretations I am able to offer, and because it gives me a form of certainty as to what is going on.

5. Transformations with "O"

The four previous sections have dealt with the path towards what is in principle an unobtainable reality, as instead we reach a reality that emerges in our psyche. They have mainly dealt with that part of reality we have grown accustomed to calling psychic and thus not the part we term material, nor with the transformations that it could conceivably engender. Since we know only what emerges in our consciousness, we cannot know for sure whether there is any real difference between the part of reality that we term psychic and the one we term material. This is not an ontological distinction but a methodological one. Ontological matter is in principle transcendental. Our transformations of psychic reality are characterized by the fact that they alter the reality they reflect. We know this when we discover that growth has taken place. We do not know for sure whether growth actually does take place at the material level. We only know about change and change is not growth. Actual material growth seems to stand in contradiction of the laws of energy, since these claim that energy and matter cannot be created or destroyed but only change in form. Qualitative growth cannot in principle be measured using quantifiable metaphors; that would be a mistake akin to attempting to measure the height of a building in decibel. Scientific transformations do not affect reality. Nobody claims that Galileo's law of falling bodies—s = 1/2gt2—affects moving objects in material reality; nor does the mathematical description of the heliocentric system move planets. However, in accepting these mathematic descriptions, giving up the old world order that saw earth as the centre and Aristotle's theory of motion, according to which flying objects long for the earth, our consciousness presumably undergoes a qualitative change. With the advent of relativistic physics, consciousness once again changed qualitatively. After Hiroshima we understand Socrates' claim that it is worse to injure than be injured, and that only a fool injures others for only fools injure themselves in a new way.

However the real growth of both collective and individual consciousness is rare and difficult, when growth is understood as a comprehensive joint insight into e.g., Socrates' statement, or Buddhist or Christian teachings of compassion. Political history demonstrates this claim with great tragedy and clarity. Few are able to stand the transformation of 40 days in the desert and even the Buddha had to make numerous lengthy detours throughout his life before he discovered the "middle road" available under his very nose.

Collective movements towards schizoid-paranoid conditions tend to recur, as is also the case in individual development. Individuals turn psychotic as do groups or collectives in the form of states. We can understand this only by presuming that the psychotic is present in all of us and that we may regress into it.

Bion expresses this movement through his Ps<=>D metaphors. Yet for every "catastrophic change" towards D, regression becomes more difficult. We can only hope that growth can continue, that we will know and not just know of. It is simply a question of whether "to be or not to be".

Notes

1. I follow Melanie Klein's use of these concepts, using the abbreviations "D" for depressive and Ps for the concept of paranoid-schizoid.
2. These two descriptive systems map psychic and physico-chemical partial realities.
3. Bion articulates a theory in "Differentiation of the psychotic from the non-psychotic personalities" (Bion 1993, pp. 45–52).
4. Jung designates this with his concepts of animus/anima and gender polarity in each individual.

5. See for example the work of Fonagy, Schore and Stern (2006).
6. Consciousness or what Kant refers to as pure apperception is more difficult to acknowledge (Bertelsen 1999).
7. Bion also refers to recall as dream-like memory and reverie (1970, p. 71), free of "memory and desire" (ibid, p. 30 ff). This pivotal distinction is central to theory of trauma and treatment in Levine 1998, pp. 189–99.
8. Author's unpublished notes.
9. Author's unpublished notes.
10. It is interesting to note that immediately after T's strong feeling of having been contained, the memory of a negative or abusive female figure recurs. I hope to analyse this in greater depth at a later point.
11. Author's unpublished notes.
12. Of course the snippets of dream and analysis offered here do not do the material full justice.
13. Bion imagines a kind of mathematics or language which describes the space of consciousness as precisely as Euclidean mathematics describe space.
14. This is obviously one of the points of *The Symposium*.
15. The concept of projective identification describes a communication between two individuals, which cannot be understood within the traditional scientific paradigm, as I/you and it/other merge. Perhaps neurological research will open up a scientific description of the phenomenon; perhaps it will be possible to scan certain brain functions during projective identification. In that event a section of psychic space and its content will be represented on a scanner in digital space.
16. In his Brazilian lectures, Bion mentions that when there are two scared people facing each other, therapy can begin.
17. Please see Section c. A Space for Growth.
18. It is well known that people have difficulty bearing both intimacy and distance. Mother and baby 'drown' in one another's gaze, but look away when they get overloaded. Both men and women chase down lovers and then chase them away.
19. Baby observation is a module in psychoanalytic training in most educational institutions in Britain. Each student follows a baby from birth to the age of two; observing the baby once a week for an hour in its daily surroundings and immediately writing a report concerning what has taken place in the inner and outer world. See also Miller et al, 1995 and Pérez-Sánchez 1990.

20. The concept of deintegration was coined by Fordham to describe a psychic condition following deliberate attentiveness (reintegration) and can be qualified as a kind of instinctual or psychoid state, where physical and psychic conditions merge. See e.g., Fordham 1976. At an early age, psychic space is created via shifts between the two states, which makes it possible to gradually perceive the world as divided into an external and an internal part (p. 22). The self arises in the tension between the two states (pp. 55 and 89 ff).
21. Small children use these mechanisms to communicate. Note the example from the baby observation where the meeting between the baby and the observer and the two of them and the mother results in grandiose pro- and introjection leading to joy etc., in the baby and observer, and where separation results in pro- and introjection leading to suffering and depression, again both in baby and observer.
22. Recent neurological research makes it possible to determine changes in different parts of the brain linked to emotions, sensations and mental activity using advanced scanning techniques. Is there a difference between brain activity and psychic activity? Certainly there is a difference between these activities and "O" as well as the language games we neurologists and therapists respectively use to interpret this activity. Perhaps there is a kind of Rosetta Stone that may communicate the contents of these languages, or a language that describes the two types of phenomena in more general terms?
23. "K" stands for knowledge, "L" for love, and "H" for hate.
24. The period following birth and the first years. The plasticity and the ability of the psyche and body to heal allow growth throughout life.
25. Author's unpublished notes.

CHAPTER THREE

Technique

Blest night of wandering,
In secret, where by none might I be spied
Nor I see anything;
Without a light or guide,
Save that which in my heart burnt in my side.

The Obscure Night of the Soul, Juan de la Cruz
(Walsh, 1920, p. 247)

a. A paradigmatic shift

Modern psychoanalysis arose within a scientific paradigm closely affiliated with medicine. The first psychoanalysts were doctors; analysts with an academic background but no medical training were termed lay analysists or non-medical analysts, and often had lower status than analysts with a medical background. The discipline of psychoanalysis borrowed status and social acceptance from the powerful advancements of medicine and natural science throughout the 1900s, where the dominant scientific paradigm had been influenced by positivist thought and method applied to a field of objects.

Bion's psychoanalysis does not abandon this paradigm. He was a soldier and a historian as well as a doctor. However, he completed or generalized this paradigm by rediscovering a immaterial inner world, inventing a space for this world and turning it into a field to which psychoanalysis can relate.[1] In consequence he created a new theory and methodology constituting the background for a general description of psychoanalytic abilities. He discovered what is termed the "analytic object", which he gave the ultimate denomination "O". He then demonstrated how this object grows into consciousness as an insight through sensation, myth and passion. This insight is on the part of both the analyst and the analysand. When it arises it becomes possible for the analyst to interpret, to "verbalize". This verbalization may be a pure echo of what has passed, in which case it is superfluous; more frequently it is an approximation, and the conversation creates a movement towards a shared insight, their shared speech and shared language temporarily creating a common myth.

The analyst and the analysand have a relationship similar to the relationship between mother and child when they are perfectly equal, sensing each other through the exchange of glances, sounds, smell, movement or rhythm, feeling each others' pain or joy. They leave this community through language—sometimes wordless—that they come to possess individually. Through this language they can perhaps continue separately into the ways in which we attempt to control each other and reality. Then they remain within the old paradigm. If therapy is successful, however, it means that two people have become able to be alone in a new way, enabling them to passionately sense the other, the world, and the self, and thereby to create new myths.

The key to the paradigmatic shift happens when the hermeneutic circle—an infinite motion towards the creation of myth—turns into a kind of non-result. "O", "becoming" or "nothing" is the focus of the work. If this movement leads to successful adjustment, work, a high income, a car, house or boat, this is of no interest. It would be better if no-one were to hear of it, since such "unfortunate" or at least unintentional results may have a tendency to arrest this infinite motion that is the very life-expression which we attempt to paraphrase through analytical work. We might fall into a dreamless sleep of cars, boats, houses etc., instead of waking up (Grotstein, 2007).

b. Techné

Techné is the Greek term for ability, referring to capabilities and actions. In this context we also extend the term to include its opposite, i.e., non-doing and inability. Thus it is the capacity for a form of absolute denial extending even to denial itself, since this also involves a form of "action" or "ability".

Bion has termed this activity "negative capability" to borrow Keats' expression for a certain state of intentional open-mindedness.[2] In therapy this is expressed through the simple fact of beginning each session by intensifying attention on the moment and initially directing it towards the body and the events unfolding around the meeting.

Obviously the therapist must be attentive both to his own body and that of the analysand. The therapist may focus by relaxing his breathing, so to speak, to fill body and thereby mind with a form of stillness. This in turn seems to create a space for the emotional change of relations, imaginings, fantasy and ideas to be unfolded and examined. Any therapist who has practiced this for a long time must remain exceedingly critical:

> The analyst's interpretations finds the analysand's personal experiences of O through detecting the L-ove, H-ate and K-nowledge linkages between analysand and analyst (infantile dependency; two-person relationship) and linkages between objects and between them and himself (Oedipal triad) (Grotstein, 2007, p. 91).

The examination of statements is a key activity in the field of philosophy. What is a statement? What does it mean to enunciate a statement? What is required in order to "judge" and what limits to or types of judgmental function or—in the case of psychoanalysis—interpretations are played out?

The limit between any kind of judgmental function and its opposite is most simply paraphrased by the dual concept of being-nothingness. Judgment then expresses "nothing" while derived from being. When the judgment expresses "nothing" it is because judgements always have multiple significations. Even so-called tautologies are bearers of meaning and hence volatilely dependent on those who attribute meaning to judgement based on "being". This may also be expressed as follows: any judgement is a transformation with a creative aspect and what is created is perishable. Only the nothingness from which creation emanates is eternal.

The earliest reflections on the being-nothingness duality may, I think, be found in the work of the pre-Socratic philosopher, Parmenides. One of Plato's main ambitions was to communicate a possible connection between these opposites. The pre-Socratics, however, were interested in "being" and were convinced that the being referred to by philosophy entailed an eternal truth. Thought and matter had not yet become sufficiently differentiated and thus eternal truth was conceived of as being at once material and immaterial. We might use the term psychoid. The fact that neurologists can now determine alterations in the brain using various scanning techniques and observe that these alterations coincide with changes in the mind as described through sensory and emotional expressions, tells us that mind and matter are but two different interpretations of the same thing. Presumably the Greek term *nous*—mind and intellect interwoven in dynamic creativity—also expresses a similar notion: Insight and being are the same (Johansen 1964, p. 169). Describing the brain using scanning technology is a verbalization of what takes place in the brain which is also articulated through poetry, myth, fairy tales, narrative, etc.

The point, however, is that psychotherapy requires not neurological, chemical or scientific descriptions, but rather mythical, poetic ones. Thus admittance is desired not into the "expression of being" of natural science or insight, but to something else. The only thing different from being is nothingness. This nothingness is in fact all that is real; this is where the good, the true and the beautiful are located; and this is what all the avenues available through language remove themselves from or evanesce in relation to. Parmenides expresses it as follows:

> ...There is need for you to learn all things—
> both the unshaken heart of persuasive [or well-rounded] Truth
> and the opinions of mortals, in which there is no true reliance.
> But nevertheless you will learn these too ...
> Come now, I will tell you—and bring away my story safely
> when you have heard it –

> the only ways of inquiry there are to think:
> the One, that it is and that it is not possible for it not to be,
> is the path of Persuasion (for it attends upon Truth),
> the other, that it is not and that it is necessary for it not to be,
> this I point out to you to be a path completely unlearnable,
> for neither may you know that which is not (for it is not to be accomplished)
> nor may you declare it.
>
> (McKirahan 1994, p. 152; Fragment 11.1, lines 28–30 and Fragment 11.2, lines 1–8)

The interpretation of this fragment is highly disputed. I suggest the simple understanding that the road to truth runs from being to non-being, where non-being is understood as a state that is obtainable only through considerable difficulty and characterized by the absence of all judgmental activity ("O"). Here the path (*hodos*) is that of the gods which we follow through what appears to be coincidence. We are drawn and guided by our passions, our will and our intuition. Plato also describes this path using a mythical story of being conveyed in a horse-drawn chariot to the house of the Gods. Parmenides greatly emphasises the fact that the "daughters of the Sun" lead the horses, while Plato underlines the force and willpower of the coachman. Perhaps horses, girls and coachman are all images of passion, intuition and willpower, while the "heart of well-rounded truth" (Phaedrus, 253c) is truly being free of the harnesses in which our mental and physical acts position being, through passion, force and intuition? Perhaps this true being should be termed nothingness or "O"?

Plato analyzes Eros throughout most of his work, understanding it as the power that drives people towards truth. Plato considers Eros a relational force that makes it possible for people to give and receive, to enter and allow entering. Eros is in every way a connective force, which operates through all senses and openings to connect, give and receive at the cellular level, the individual level and at the collective or social level. The value of the result is not conditioned by what "openings" permit the meeting, but through transformation itself or the creative activity that arises. "Becoming" is "Eros".

In the *Symposium*, Diotima is the great master of the art leading to the discovery of the non-polar, non-dual (Plato's *Symposium*

210d; Bertelsen, 2003). Plato lets the participants move towards this absolute infinite place through their various speeches to Eros. The roads are many. Phaedrus and Pausanias discuss these roads—and their pitfalls—through personal and social relations of a sexual or educational character. Eryximachus describes the road of science and the art of healing. Aristophanes describes the road of myth or poetry. Socrates, however, makes the words of Diotima present in his speech, a kind of abstraction of nothingness and the stages leading to nothingness, after describing the multiple expressions of creativity in sexuality, friendship and social life. The teacher-pupil relationship between Socrates and Diotima is the consummation. I think the results of this meeting are what Bion indicates as the results of a meeting with "O".

The underlying values of our culture are deeply anchored in this very form of *techné*; discovering "O". This is repeated in Christianity and is perhaps most clearly expressed the gospel according to Thomas:

> When you make the two one, and you make the inside as the outside and the outside as the inside and the above as the below, and if you establish the male with the female as a single unity so that the man will not act masculine and the woman not act feminine, when you establish an eye in the place of an eye and a hand in the place of a hand and a foot in the place of a foot: an image in the place of an image!— then shall you enter [the Sovereignty]. (Logion 22, Gospel of Thomas Hypertext Interlinear, http://www.metalog.org/files/th_interlin/th022.html)

In Western culture, however, there have been long periods—we are in fact in the midst of such a period now—where being has been confused with nothingness. We mistakenly assume that our own creations are true, real and good. We dance around our golden calves of science and everyday occupations, forgetting that all our creations are subject to the law of annihilation or perhaps rather the law of reversal or change.

The road towards that insubstantiality we mistakenly call being is in many ways important and necessary, while being simply what it is, i.e., a kind of wakeful dream that in principle has the same illusory nature as the dreams we experience while asleep.

c. Memory and desire

Bion emphasizes that the process of working towards a state of no illusions between analyst and analysand is not "sub-scientific" but rather super-scientific; "O" is within reach and thus transformation or creation and growth can take place.

In this respect Bion is in complete agreement with Freud, in his intense preoccupation with demonstrating psychoanalysis to be a scientific discipline (Freud, 1950). Thus Freud repeatedly emphasized that the nucleus or depths encompassed in every scientific activity is an intuition or a form of beholding of truth, where this truth so to speak captures the scientist who makes himself open to capture. Freud described this process of making oneself open using the term free flowing attention (Bion, 1992). It was in this openness that Joseph Breuer, while working with Freud, discovered determinants of nervous ailments in a patient. Determinants tended to confuse the doctors, who mistake the symptoms with the actual disease.

Freud targeted these determinants, formulating his theory—or rather his numerous theories—around them. Here Freud reached the core of his self-analysis or his own "self-reflection", which consists precisely in seeking to open oneself. Freud obtained the ability of insight; technically capable of being "free flowing attention", whence he offered help to his patients.

Both the use and the understanding of free flowing attention require experience in advanced psychoanalytical methodology, achieved through analysis. Few are capable of completing this work without the aid of a "master" as Freud was obliged to.

I have previously attempted to point out that memory can be considered both recall and reminiscence. Reminiscence is discovering a condition that may be mentalised through interpretation. For example we may find that a certain smell causes a feeling of discomfort that we may explain by referring to a certain event. Conversely we may describe an event and discover a sudden sensation of well-being or discomfort as a sensing or some kind of bodily vibration.[3]

Both cases are phenomena from the past that reach the conscious area of attention through distortions or what I have termed transformations. What Bion terms "without memory and desire" is that which is located prior to both memory and reminiscence and is free of any pleasant or unpleasant connotations.

In other words this is a state of consciousness aimed at neither past nor future, in fact not aimed at anything at all. The radicality of this postulate is evident in that intentionality is frequently emphasized as the essence of consciousness, although Bion disavows this in his understanding of the characteristics of consciousness.

Thus real creativity and the super-scientific may be found in those places that are devoid of mental intentionality.

One of the strengths of therapy is that judgements and statements are formulated while the observations are going on. Thus they are ideally linked to the "moments" in which they come into existence, which they "are". They are part of them. The present moment and every reaction to it, be it denial, affirmation or annihilation is what constitutes therapy. In order to allow this moment to come through as purely as possible, it is essential that it be distorted as little as possible. This is the reason consciousness must be liberated of every form of direction stemming from the past or targeting the future. One might say that "remembering" retains consciousness in the past while "desiring" directs it towards the future. Thus the present moment is controlled; one might say it is spun out between cause and motive. Freud very precisely defines this state of consciousness that is open and creative as "free-floating". This free-floating condition is also what permits access to being or the so-called unconscious.

Reminiscing, remembering, wishing or desiring—i.e., both memory and desire—are sensually or emotionally connected to form a unit. This is precisely the reason why these states must be banned from therapeutic space since they fill up consciousness with archaeological material; a form of garbage that prevents the psychic contents of consciousness from rejuvenating themselves—or even from becoming visible at all. Psychic objects are not material things; hence they cannot be smelled, tasted, seen or touched. They have no form in space. They are special objects in that psychic space that—if filled with reminiscences and remembered things—hide and distort this very space, preventing its true, creative nature from unfolding by creating new content, conditions and structures of consciousness out of "nothing".

Consciousness has a tendency to fill up. It is infinitely greedy and does not voluntarily desist from its acquisitive activities. Consciousness itself is invisible due to all this content, just as the trees obscure the forest itself. We cling to this content, thereby failing to cross the threshold that prevents us from feeling the particular character of consciousness itself.

Perhaps anxiety is the most terrible of the guardians of this threshold. However, sleepiness, desire, arrogance, laziness, miserliness and envy also colour the contents of consciousness, thereby preventing its actual being from becoming present in the field of attention.

No doubt the therapeutic work required to reach this openness is extremely anxiety-provoking for both the analyst and the analysand, who both seek this condition since this is where change or growth may occur. When both feel liberated of obligatory therapeutic aims such as being "cured" or becoming "normal" or "fit for work", they feel less guilt if they do not succeed, or for that matter, if they do. The material that arises in therapy becomes more fresh and vital and the order in which it does so ceases to matter.

It has been essential for me to consider the theoretical position assumed by therapists—and occasionally defended with incomprehensive rigidity—as part of a larger puzzle, whose eventual interrelation becomes an interesting possibility to be discovered as required. However this puzzle is only indirectly related to what goes on between the analyst and the analysand. The pieces of the puzzle—all the various theories—are possible transformations of a reality that *was* theirs. But what should be kept in focus is the new reality arising from transformation or growth. This does not in any way mean that therapy is a discipline devoid of theory. On the contrary, the therapists must be exceedingly sure of their theoretical knowledge of the nooks and recesses of the mind; so sure that they do not need them when abroad in the mind. So sure in fact, that they immediately realize when they are moving into uncharted territory and into reality. After all, human beings cannot function without a system of reference of some sort to help position ourselves. The theories are not meant, however, to describe the reality of the clinical situation, but rather to create a secure system of reference for the therapist, thus making it more bearable move into the unknown where the analysand's potential for growth may be found.

When this succeeds both parts of the therapeutic couple experience greater freedom, higher energy and more nuances in their emotional options. Quite simply, both are able to contain greater parts of themselves and the other and perhaps even of others. This also means that fantasy-lives and imagerial representations become less colourful and less nuanced, permitting psychic conditions to appear more clearly with fewer layerings of object-representations (Bion, 1992).

These conditions are known and described by all who have speculated on becoming or creativity. Bion's favourite example of this was the poet Keats, who refers to this state as "negative capability".

However, it is also quite precisely described by mystics, who experience the world as anything but mystical, since they believe they have knowledge of precisely the good, true and beautiful which characterises the proper mode of being of consciousness.

To those who have become able to entirely abandon memory and desire and banish the particular greed of consciousness, consciousness appears as pure love, compassion, trust and gratitude. This is most likely what Kierkegaard refers to as the religious stage, which it is probably not possible to inhabit all the time.

Those parts of consciousness that function as neurotic or psychotic, rational or irrational are learned. They maintain our life-situations. If new situations are to come into existence—perhaps because there are unconducive aspects of those currently being practiced—these learned modes of functioning must be unlearned. We must be liberated of the enforced modes to which we have been subjugated and with which we have learned to function. This applies both individually and socio-psychologically.

As children we are free of unconducive aspects of the cultural burden. While we must not become as children once more, we do need to unlearn the unconducive and archaic forms of this burden. At least we must attempt to seek insight into this burden that might also more biblically be termed "Original Sin".

One of the most decisive concepts for any therapist is the ability to carry out acts of faith, i.e., an act expressing a leap into depths unknown, where security is lacking and paradoxes reign (Bion, 1970).[4]

Bion terms this event column F. The abstraction of an event or action is "concept" and may then assume various forms as expressed in the horizontal axis of the "Grid" either through definitions, psi (lies), notation, attention, examination (Oedipus) or action. F cannot, in principle, be described, since every form of description is an action that is a movement away from F. Thus F is an expression of "O" or shapeless substance, just as consciousness is to the mystic.

Where the concept of an 'act of faith' implies, a mode of action or a conscious quantity the concepts of contained-contain ("♂♀") would rather seem to indicate a state or a quality of consciousness.

Thus therapeutic method or work has both a qualitative and a quantitative side.

The concept "♂♀" indicates quite precisely an aspect of psychoanalytic method. It is a well-known metaphor in Christian and Buddhist religious mysticism. The icons of these religions are not alchemical signs, as they are to Bion, but rather use the metaphor of the human body. Consider the image of the Rucellai Madonna, painted by Italian master Duccio di Buoninsegna, in which Mary is depicted housing the congregation (Hartt, 1994), or of the yab-yum images of Samantabhadra and Samantabhadri in sexual union. Consider Mary holding the dead Jesus in Michelangelo's "Pietà", or images of Mary breastfeeding the infant Jesus. Containing or contained and being connected is the deeper, anchored meaning of psychoanalytic work, but so is the fact that this is work we must carry out in loneliness. There is no escaping this paradox; it is what sets us in motion.

However, it also makes our path difficult since we must not rest in the formal. The path breaks down all hierarchical structures and yet it can only occur where such structures exist.

d. Philosophy, therapy, or the truth drive

Philosophy means love of insight. This is a passion that seeks to see something non-objective internally. This quest is eternal and never-ending and does not rest on its laurels. It refuses to settle. The philosophers of antiquity frequently travelled around, offering people part in their insight; they were known as Peripatetics, i.e., those who wander around.

There is no clear semantic definition of therapy. However, the name is known from a group of people who joined together in their everyday lives to seek the good life, both inwardly and outwardly through social relations. In antiquity they frequently lived a little distance outside the towns, whence they offered treatment for other people's sufferings while they themselves lived the life their treatment would procure for those who sought it.

In modern times, philosophy has become a professional activity. We speak of the practice of philosophy by teachers in classrooms and in relation to university curricula, syllabi and professional standards. Philosophers assist in the strategic work of corporations, i.e., drawing up ethical accounts. In brief, philosophy and philosophers have been enrolled in the army of modernity to carry out things. This has always been a temptation for philosophers. Even Plato himself fell for this temptation when he went to Syracuse as political advisor to the tyrant Dion. He thus hoped to transfer his ideas of goodness, truth and beauty in society from their absolute being in conscious space into the world of phenomena, drawing them in from a being-space or a nothingness-state. Naturally this experiment was destined to fail in the state of Syracuse, because of the immanence of insufficiency, negation and change. The experiment itself, however, was philosophical, since it emanated from the truth drive that is the innermost core of philosophy. The result was philosophically insignificant.

Perhaps the experiment in Syracuse was this truth drive itself, just as therapy is as it unfolds between analyst and analysand. Therapy expresses the truth drive.

Just as philosophers have become professional philosophers, therapists have become professional therapists. In so doing both the philosopher and the therapist distance themselves from that which is essential, namely living the life of the philosopher and the therapist in the here and now, in the company of those who seek the insights that arise from their way of life.

Therapists beg not to be blinded by their potential and ever so infinitely unstable results. They do not want to hear of them to avoid falling asleep from the ceaseless prodding of the truth drive. Resting on one's laurels is one way of going to sleep. These proddings or rather the frustrations that arise from them must be endured since they are the source of that constant creative stream, that renewal of consciousness that is life.

Doctors, conversely, have a radically different goal. Their desire is to heal, ease and help the patient very often according to specific ends as specified in societal norms or values. Thus it is unfortunate to mix the art of healing with therapy, even though both may be beneficial.

Bion refers to the oedipal triangle both as factually and desirably present as a model for all therapeutic sessions; thus that which takes place in therapy becomes personal verbalizations or conceptualizations of a three-way relationship. This three-way relationship is understood in multiple dimensions: as the relation between the senses, the conscious and the unconscious, or between the senses, intuition and pre-concepts. These three-way opposites create the structures of therapeutic sessions and these are then either verbalised or carried into the outside world through whatever other relations in which the parties may participate (Bion, 1984). The Oedipal myth and its individual components are a kind of holographic image of consciousness since myth is what produces the prodding, frustration or truth drive, as a beginning, a middle and an end. Consider the Sphinx, in possession of the riddle, its solution and Thebes. Oedipus has something more than this, namely the truth drive. It kills the Sphinx, but in the long run it also destroys Oedipus just as it created him. It frees the Thebes of the plague but also occasions its return.

Philosophers are people who have thrown themselves into the arms of the truth drive, effectively leaving themselves at its mercy. Their lives and their circumstances express this. They strive to be one with the truth as well as to express it. In order to create personal growth for themselves and their analysands, therapists must subject themselves to the same search for truth. This means that therapists must become identical with certain aspects of their analysands in order to express these aspects as their own and consequently to alter them prior to returning them in their modified form.

Grotstein writes: "The analyst must become the analysand's passion (emotion) and overcome it by dreaming it. He must experience it and transcend it—evolve it from P-S to D" (Grotstein, 2007, p. 91; Bion, 1992, pp. 287–91).

Naturally truth is not changed through this transformation of consciousness. Truth and reality can never be changed. Rather the consciousness seeking truth and reality must modify itself through a series of changes. Truth is the feeling of being rightly possessed of oneself in the form of one's own feelings. This takes place when personal filters in the form of sense and the senses modify or create the contents of consciousness through a process of approach and acquisition. This is a life-long process.

I previously termed this process the hermeneutic circle: Here I am trying to demonstrate that it does in fact take place. In the section in Chapter Two on transformations I attempted to illustrate how this may happen. In Chapter Four I shall attempt to show where. But the "that", "how" and "where" is everywhere, even between the lines.

e. On frameworks and their disruption

The therapeutic technique outlined in the previous section is difficult to acquire. There is significant support to be found for those enduring the paradoxes of this way of working in a number of simple rules applicable to the professional meeting between analyst and analysand. The noblest goal of therapy is self-insight and perhaps this is the decisive goal. Such insight is naturally not reached purely in therapy but in all aspects of life. In therapy it is important to uphold the therapeutic framework since this focuses attention on that shared inner space of consciousness in which all development takes place. When this framework has become sufficiently stable to contain devotion, security, respect and friendliness and their opposites—arrogance, anger, condescension and doubt—the actual work can begin. In other words, the framework serves the purpose of allowing both parties to completely relax their minds as well as their bodies and set free all emotions. There must be sufficient security to enable the observation and verbalization of all stagings that may occur in therapy—particularly those that take place in the room and in connection with therapy sessions. "Here-and-now" interventions or interpretations express this goal.

The purpose of the framework is to insert both parties to therapy in an equal, symmetric relationship in spite of the fact that both are at risk of receding into the infantilely dependent layers of their consciousness. In other words, both people present in this space must firmly continue trying to be independent adults to become able to see all the infantile events playing out in and for therapy, and attempt to consider them symbolically. Together the two parties can then discuss what is conducive and what is not.

In therapy there are two anxious children present—in addition to the adult parts—and both are fighting to be adult. The therapeutic framework is the agreement entered into by the two adult parts, to which they both adhere in spite of the fact that it may appear better and easier to become like the children they have constructed and with whom they have identified throughout their childhood.

Therapy works with these constructions to seek new ones that function in a more conducive manner.

To me as a therapist, being an adult usually means respecting agreements, be they appointment schedules, hours, payment and social conventions. A contract is entered into and upheld. Part of this contract involves an agreement as to how and under what circumstances therapy or the contract will be terminated.

To me the infantile lies in accepting ones dependency on the therapist while assigning the therapist responsibility for oneself. In other words the infantile means giving up on a commensal relationship in this respect and losing oneself for good in a new symbiotic or parasitic form.[5]

Payment is a decisive part of this structure: clients pay for what they receive and therapists receive payment for what they provide. We are dealing with an exchange where two independent individuals make each their equally valid contribution. There is no shortage of attacks on this adult form. Therapists may feel that they are underpaid and perhaps unappreciated both socially and in their therapeutic relationships. Clients may feel they are being financially exploited, do not get their problems resolved, while they feel that they are inferior and deem the therapist to be incompetent. In cases where payment does not enter into the equation—for instance in the therapies offered through the public health care system—the equality of the therapeutic relationship must be established in what is perhaps a somewhat more difficult manner: Patients must be made to respect and understand that they are contributing when they come, see, hear or speak and when they see, feel or interpret states pertaining to themselves or to others. In any case, these mutual contributions are significant. Later this equality may be extended to include the exchange of those abstractions of true relations that take the form of money.

The interplay around the sessions is equally symbolic. Appointments are changed, cancelled, postponed. Therapists are sought at odd hours and receive phone calls out of session. Interruptions imposed by holidays are angrily protested and these feelings of dependency and betrayal may be subsequently demonstrated by tardiness, failing to show up, rejection and passive or active—internally or externally targeted—anger, silence or offence.

It is evident that what is taking place in these interplays is a continuous transgression of the borders between adult and child followed by their re-establishment. The adult and the childish aspects meet and become known to one another both in oneself and in the other. This process of breaking down and rebuilding trains a conscious acceptance of one's own borders as well as those of the therapist. Borders are furthermore understood as transitions between acceptance/rejection or betrayal; respect/disrespect of one self and of the other; and also as the polarized feelings of loneliness or solitude and relation or togetherness. We can bear loneliness, but only through our awareness of the possibility of togetherness, be it in the form of dream, fantasy or faith. We see the other and feel his or her consciousness but only because we are ourselves with our own consciousness.

It is hardly comprehensible why these processes take such a long time to unfold. Perhaps the cause should be sought in an understandable apprehension towards all things new and unfamiliar. After all, we know those borders with which we have become accustomed to live, although we may repeatedly experience the limitations they impose on us. How are we to know that moving the fence posts will not make everything much worse? Let us make sure we move them only inch by tiny inch. Indeed for the most part such innate caution appears perfectly sensible.

Hopefully while these games are playing out the therapist is the most adult and attentive party to the process.

f. Contain/Contained or "O"

Early psychoanalysts formulated quite precise descriptions of projective and introjective mechanisms. Karl Abraham, whom Melanie Klein worked for in Berlin, has described these mechanisms in his studies on melancholia, and Klein herself first formulated her description of projective identification in "Notes on some schizoid mechanisms" (Klein, 1975). She considered this mechanism an unconscious, intra-psychic pathological defence, where a person—in his or her imagination—may manipulate another, causing him or her—often unwittingly—to enter into a form of manipulated state.[6] Bion discovered that all these mechanisms were ways of creating relations and expressed the understanding that their purpose was to permit people to declare themselves to one another. He considered these mechanisms to be abilities or properties common to us all, like other biological mechanisms which serve to maintain life, such as eating and eliminating, in- and exhaling, seeing and being seen, listening and speaking, smell and smelling, and coitus.

Throughout all of these processes the persons trade roles. First one person is a space or container for parts of the other, then one person is partially contained in the other. In these processes, it is easy to get the impression that what you contain is your own, something given to you and then something that you are returning or perhaps divesting yourself of. You might even be utterly devoid of insight or understanding as regards these processes, as with other metabolic processes. They simply take place of their own accord.

Since Euclidian space is well-defined, there is no difficulty in understanding that air can be split into O_2 and CO_2 through the process of breathing, to be subsequently spread throughout this space both locally within the body and less locally through the air that is exhaled and moves into the atmosphere. The non-objects in the form of the emotions of which we communicate using the mechanism of projective identification also split into individual spaces contained in persons and merge in the psychic space I shall attempt to define more closely in Chapter four. In a way all people share the emotions in that space. From here they can enter the attention aimed at intra- or extra-psychic delimitations of this space. Attention then creates what is alternately containing and contained: psychic objects, their relations and delimitations. The important thing is that all objects are distorted by attention as they come into being (Bion, 1992).

Grotstein has termed Klein's model of projective identification a "one-person" model while calling Bion's a "two-person" model. The model I am attempting to specify here is a three-way model which I believe to be implied in Bion's epistemology or in his theories on thought (Grotstein, 2007).

The best realization of this model lies in the experiences of the mother-child relationship. The three parties here are "mother", "child", and "O".

Babies have thoughts, emotions or feelings that are as yet unthought. They share these with their mother, who while not necessarily thinking them has developed tools throughout her own childhood, enabling their thinking. The mother contains these thoughts and emotions with the baby and articulates them. Bion refers to the channels for this articulation as "reverie", alpha-function, dreams or fantasies. When mothers do not have the appropriate channels of articulation at their disposal—which they do not always, or they may be present to varying degrees—no processing takes place or it may be insufficient. This places a burden on the communication which in the worst-case scenario fails to take place, which means that no projections take place. There is non-communication. Difficult or terrible feelings are not processed by the mother and seek other channels. They may turn into crying, screaming, extreme activity or into passive suffering, fantasies and somatisations. When they remain un-thought or unarticulated in the baby they fill it like so much garbage, impossible to bear or get rid of. The baby becomes the dumping-ground for "O". Bion calls this garbage "beta-elements"; unprocessed psychic impressions.

Grotstein writes:

> The source of the analyst's transformations is from within his own repertoire of experiences and emotions, which he seems to match up (simulate) with those of the analysands and become the "O" (the unknown and unknowable truth) of the session (Bion, 1965/1984, p. 146). My understanding of what Bion means by this is that the analyst must recruit his own self-activated simulation of the analysand's experience and *become* it as thoroughly as possible Thus, the source of the analyst's information is largely from within himself, but it is my opinion that it also emerges from the mystery of projective-introjective transmission process detailed earlier (Grotstein, 2007, p. 183; Bion, 1984, p. 146).

Grotstein refers to Damasi who has expressed the opinion to him, that people are able to create within themselves feelings and emotions that are virtually identical to those of their fellow beings. This takes place through the learned function of empathy, which grows out of community, initially with the parents and later with all who form part of a life-long network of relations.

To my mind it appears to be a beneficial simplification to postulate a common space for the emotions and feelings that are objectified here. People share a space of common consciousness with common emotions developed communally and on which we depend. Each individual is at all times fully responsible for this entire space.

If consensus could be reached on this point, projective-introjective transmission would no longer be a mystery, but a reality, just as obvious as different types of metabolic activity involving the ingestion of necessary sustenance and the rejection of the superfluous.

g. Becoming a psychotherapist

Anyone wishing to become a therapist must engage in at least four equally significant fields of study.

1. Personal reflection or personal experience

This is a form of self-development where one's own encounters, victories and defeats constitute the material. This work should be supported through individual therapy, possibly supplemented by some form of group therapy.

2. Clinical experience

This is where encounters with others seeking help in various ways constitute the material of one's experiences and reflection. This work should be supported by others in various forms of supervision.

3. Theoretical knowledge

This is where constructions built by oneself and by others on the basis of experiences obtained through personal or clinical experience are formalised. This knowledge is primarily obtained through teaching and studying and may provide distraction, consolation and inspiration in working both with oneself and with others. It is essential that these studies are not limited to individual disciplines like psychology, medicine, biochemistry or theology, but unfold in different cultural constructions: poetry, fiction and art are decisive theoretical constructions and hence constitute fields of experience for the symbolizing creativity of consciousness. Most theoretical constructions are described in analytical literature.

For me the pieces of wreckage which survivors of a shipwreck cling to symbolize our theoretical constructs. Just like survivors swimming in the infinite ocean of consciousness we reach for our theoretical constructs to stay afloat, and for rest and consolation.

We cling to them, but only to start swimming in the infinite again. We may learn to frolic in the waters of consciousness like dolphins.

4. Learning to maintain aloneness even in the encounter

The best model of training imaginable to strengthen this ability appears to me to be the kind of baby observation seminars that are obligatory at a number of training institutes. This model includes the seminars held by Esther Bick and Martha Harris with a number of other Kleinian therapists as an obligatory part of the initial study-program in the 1950s. Termed the Tavistock model, this consists of a group of students who meet ordinary mothers with ordinary babies in their daily surroundings on a weekly basis to observe what is happening. Once a month, the group meets with a supervisor to discuss the weekly observations of their individual infants.

The observations include external as well as internal states and events. After every session featuring mother and child or another carer, careful notes are made of "everything" that has taken place. These notes form the basis of discussions at the monthly seminars. The sessions run until the child turns two.

Following the in-depth description carried out by people like Fonagy, Stern & Schore (2006) in their affect-studies and their studies of child development, we now have a far more precise idea of what takes place in the soma as well as in the psyche through the encounters and moments of the spaces unfolding in the mother-child dyad. It now appears evident that the therapist's own infantile wounds present an obstacle to functioning at an optimum level with the client. Similarly factors surrounding the client's mother-child dyad must be assumed to create the greater part of his or her problematics. Hence it is of course enormously significant that therapists obtain a clear and precise sense of precisely these infantile conditions through their education. Presumably their impact is also felt in cases of transference and in the creation of the synergies experienced in therapeutic space. When these infantile states are intra-psychically observed in the therapist, created into the interpersonal dynamic (mother-child-observer) and interpersonally experienced and discussed with fellow students under the supervision of a teacher—i.e., in an empirically scientific context—the training process—in my opinion—becomes sufficiently well-founded and only then does the training process provide the ideal framework to support future therapists.

Mother-child observation seminars model the Oedipal framework in which all therapy takes place in a setting spun out between the analyst in the role of the mother, the analysand as the child and the supervisor, colleagues, and the entire professional field as observers.

Institutions as well as the analytic process involve numerous games along the lines of *folies à deux*. When such *folies* are contained growth is created. Therapists or institutions are affected by pupils or analysands. This might be described as the unconscious fantasies of the analysands being projected into the therapist. However, we must assume that both parties unconsciously preserve these fantasies and that the two consciousnesses provide a kind of mutual response in that they affect each other. Perhaps the theory of mirror neurons is a kind of response to a theory of *folies à deux*. What we see is that individual consciousnesses are being immanently tuned to produce the same images.

> ...the analyst ... becomes that unconscious aspect of himself that is always already dormant within him resonantly and which always *potentially* corresponds to the analysand's projected emotions (Grotstein, 2007, p. 186).

It is important to emphasize that the same consciousness is working and at work in all people and that as such it would be fallacious to refer to individuals or institutions as possessing an abnormal consciousness. The only abnormality must thus pertain to the mode of functioning of consciousness or of its contents.

For therapists, or indeed for anyone participating in such a seminar, there are opportunities for healing and insight into that which was perhaps not ideal in their own mother-child dyad. The interpersonal integrative mechanism can change throughout life if we so desire and if we decide to facilitate this. This has been convincingly demonstrated by Fonagy, Schore and Stern (2006).

The essential goal for therapists must be to train the ability to recognize and to impose limits between infantile and adult aspects in themselves and their clients. Attacks on these borders are violent, frequent and inscrutable. They affect the emotions described above and there is a danger of breaking down the framework, meaning that therapy may be terminated in an inappropriate time or in an inappropriate way. The common human space of consciousness must be known, in the same way as the fisherman and the fish must know the sea. It is no good if therapists—like the sailors who sailed with Columbus—are increasingly afraid of falling into hell as they approach what they believe to be the boundaries of space. They must know or trust that there are no such boundaries.

Freud has used the discipline of archaeology as a model of the work unfolding in therapy and Bion—equally inspired by Freud—used medicine. Archaeology and medicine reside in two distinct scientific paradigms: the hermeneutic and the scientific. The scientific rules that develop within the philosophies of science and that are rendered utilizable in various ways in different professional sciences constitute the framework that must be respected in therapy. The therapeutic process draws equally on both paradigms. The constructs of therapy glean their forms from all scientific paradigms and disciplines, be it in the form of causally determined explanations or prognoses that respect known logical forms and empirical demands of verification or falsification, or in the form of narrative constructions that must be coherent as well as in accordance with current rules of truth and probability as they are applied in archaeology, history and literature.

Notes

1. See Chapter four.
2. Expressed in a letter to George and Thomas Keats, dated Sunday, 21 December, 1817, as well as in poems such as *La Belle Dame Sans Merci* (1819).
3. See Chapter one.
4. This opus treats method and technique. Concerning ♂♀ see pp. 106–129.
5. See Chapter four.
6. See Chapter two, section e.

CHAPTER FOUR

Symbols, models or analogies

Previously I have attempted to outline Bion's thought as I see it by describing and utilizing some of his concepts that effectively seek to delimit an ontological prerequisite for psychic elements, i.e., a space to contain them. Bion has seen or seized this space and acknowledged that it may best be described through the relations between psychic objects, where these objects behave in a regular manner reminiscent of objects in Euclidian or physical space, when these are described in the language of mathematics. Hence physical and psychic spaces exist as a form of parallel worlds. After all physical space is also described through the connections existing between physical objects such as galaxies, planets, atoms, etc. Bion believes that the task of psychoanalytic science is to expand our knowledge of the structures, regularities and patterns that exist in this psychic space and to seek out a form of mathematics to more precisely determine these experiments, for which his minutely detailed descriptions lay the groundwork.

His concepts, symbols and invariants represent structures, relations and entities in this space, as do physical and mathematical formulae in Euclidian space. Bion's attempts are distinct from previous attempts made in the fields of psychology, theology, art and literature mainly by their level of abstraction. Fairy tales and myths hence also try to illuminate Ps<=>D; and also attempt in cases such as the myths of Original Sin, the Tower of Babel, or Oedipus to describe several invariants in psychic space. All of these myths and numerous fairy tales describe opposition to growth or transformations in "O" and the pain and anxiety associated with such growth.

The theoretical systems utilized in psychotherapy are of a scientific nature not immediately identical to the empiric or inductive sciences, although the similarities are greater than the differences. A thorough description of this theme would be an extensive undertaking but I shall nevertheless strike a few relevant chords.

Scientific activity sees truth as its goal. Yet goal and activity must be kept separate, since truth is a borderline concept that can never be attained by science. The concept is transcendental in character: if a science claims that its results are true, this in itself is invalidating since science as it is must then cease as the activity it is, i.e., a search. Scientific being is searching or becoming, not appropriation. It is possible to seek or test scientifically, but the results are principally short-lived. As products they are of course sometimes important, good and beautiful and at others nasty, ugly and evil. Modern science, after all, was what made it possible to exterminate 6 million Jews during World War II and to bomb Hiroshima. Unfortunately the change in consciousness that scientific results brought about in, e.g., Einstein and Bohr, were not realized in the same way as their material opportunities for destruction (Bohr, 1959).[1] Similarly the results of medico-science bring about countless examples of barbarism instead of compassion, in spite of what are fortunately the best of intentions.

Psychoanalysis and other forms of therapy do not consist of their theoretic results but of the activity unfolding in the therapeutic space between the therapist and the analysand. Sciences are all too frequently confused with their products or even by-products/side-effects such as knowledge, theories, structure, concepts, possibilities for control, the utilization of power, or predictive opportunities.

Today science is often used to create hierarchies and systems of power, both of which are utterly at odds with its essential character.

In the case of psychotherapy, the therapeutic effect is a side-effect. This is also the case because this highly esteemed effect is frequently associated with becoming high-functioning in a manner determined by society. This amounts to simple manipulation, devoid of ethical or scientific considerations, where what works is not necessarily true nor at all scientific. For instance, placebos are highly effective, and therapeutic and medicinal treatments alike can be useful, although we frequently do not know whether the actual treatments are causing the effect rather than something else entirely. When a treatment works it is considered good enough and the therapist may feel satisfied; however, these "good-enough" consequences have nothing to do with the possible scientific aims of psychoanalysis or medicine.

The scientific search is invalidated if short-sighted individual value-targets are permitted to limit it. This does not, of course, mean, that we should dispose of applied science altogether. For therapy as science it has been fortunate that the use of therapy often leads to a lessening of the sufferings of the client or the patient. Freud's medical background ensured a link between psychoanalysis and the ancient goals of doctors, namely to help, ease and occasionally heal, but never to do harm.[2] This has created a stream of therapy patients, which permits therapists to make a living from therapeutic work. In reality, this activity has been a search for a deeper truth of humanity, and its external success in helping—and sometimes healing—has enabled a deeper goal: that search for truth which is the core meaning of therapy. We do not know for sure, whether it is the search *per se*, or the knowledge it creates that helps clients. I myself am inclined to the belief that the searching attention the therapist directs towards the client is what constitutes the effective element of treatment. This attention must be distinguished from whatever ensuing results may be published. I wonder how much of medical therapy "works" through the attention doctors give patients and the feelings created by the doctor-patient relationship (Andersen et al. 1997).

The confusion created by the existence of this highly effective goal in our work must be kept separate from any scientific goals we might have. This applies in the humanities a well as in the natural sciences. We cannot reject science for rendering possible the production of atomic bombs. We cannot reject the production of medicine for the lethality of overdoses. What we can do is demand sobriety, which means requiring the continued separation of theory and practice. Such sobriety implies a division between knowledge and power. The corruptive capacity is equally applicable to the sciences, and great power leads to great corruption. Absolute power, for which many would abuse science, leads to absolute corruption.

a. The "Grid" as a symbol or tool in psychoanalysis

I understand the "Grid" as an attempt to pin down the possible contents of psychoanalytic space, thereby defining this infinite space in and of itself. It is an attempt to create a double definition, a kind of binocular vision of the psyche. One "eye" runs vertically, from the concrete to abstract version of various thought-types. This axis also represents the tension between Hate and Love, where row A is mainly Hate and row H is mainly Love. The other "eye" runs horizontally, expressing usage and/or action understood as the utilization or action of thoughts through the organ of consciousness. Hence thoughts are "matter" processed through the action of thinking. All this takes place in consciousness, which is not located in Euclidian space, having instead this space as a kind of third "eye" or co-ordinate of the psychic space we are present in—and share—with all existing life, as is the case with Euclidian space.

Both spaces feature a kind of mutual dependency between the space itself and its contents. Growth, then, is the knowledge or awareness that change has taken place in this space, where space and consciousness constitute a kind of double definition, a kind of synonyms. This knowledge is expressed in the "Grid" on the vertical axis as degrees of abstraction and on the horizontal as a state or activity of consciousness. I think that both ultimate activity and ultimate abstraction are "O". "O" cannot be determined but may be approached through infinite love, goodness, and beauty.

Both the space of consciousness as determined through a dyad, and the contents of this space as determined through object relations function as determining metaphors or concepts in psychology.[3] Discovering this has the same significance as I imagine the discovery of the circulatory system described by Harvey in the 18th century. The body became a "circulatorily-structured" space whose vital processes might be investigated, just as the psyche will become a "relationally-structured" space whose vital processes may likewise be examined, and which in addition "is" this investigation.[4]

Bion's Grid

		Definitory Hypotheses	Psi	Notation	Attention	Inquiry	Action	n,
A	beta elements	A1	A2				A6	
B	alpha elements	B1	B2	B3	B4	B5	B6	Bn
C	Dream Thoughts	C1	C2	C3	C4	C5	C6	Cn
D	Pre conception	D1	D2	D3	D4	D5	D6	Dn
E	Conception	E1	E2	E3	E4	E5	E6	En
F	Concept	F1	F2	F3	F4	F5	F6	Fn
G	Scientific Deductive System		G2					
H	Algebraic Calculus							

Figure 4.1. The Grid.

Horizontal Axis = modifications of reality								
		Definitory Hypotheses	Psi	Notation	Attention	Inquiry	Action	n,
Vertical Axis = categorisations of reality, psi-categories								
A	Beta elements							
B	Alpha elements: concrete thinking, bizarre objects, nameless dread							
C	Dream Thoughts: dreams, myths, stories, religious systems, literature							
D	Pre-conception							
E	Conception							
F	Concept							
G	Scientific Deductive Systems, systematised educational structures, codifications, etc.							
H	Algebraic Calculus							

Figure 4.2. The Grid with modifications.

1. The horizontal axis

In the following I shall try to describe the different forms of reality modification which the Horizontal Axis seeks to express.

They take place when the mother so to speak through her reverie function dilutes the frustrations experienced by the baby either at the breast or elsewhere. This may take place through various forms of psychic activity that alter the sensual stimuli from their originally form and turn them into mental representations. Hence this axis expresses modes of action. It expresses transformations or acts of creation that take place in consequence of the contraction expressed by Bion's alpha function in the claim that materially sensible things may be transformed into something mental.

The attempt of dream work to express emotional content through images may be the best analogy to the work performed by the alpha function.

The following observations in relation to a baby-observation may illustrate the working mode of the alpha function. The sensory physical discomfort of the mother and baby during feeding at one breast becomes the mental image of suffering in a "slip of the tongue" of the observer, where blood, not milk, flows from the breast.

February 8, 1994. Nursing, breastfeeding

> During this activity, the child seems to be in symbiosis with the mother. The child's eyes are open at the first observations and the mother looks into his eyes, but she does not see. Mother and child seem lost in each other, immersed in the same ocean. The child sucks energetically and the experience appears sometimes violent, sometimes gently caressing. A world of experience is exchanged. There is a difference between the two breasts from the very beginning. The mother has suffered a cracked nipple on one side and was in pain whenever the child nursed from this breast. There have been no problems on the other side. Nursing begins with the intact nipple and satisfied, the child lies, relaxed on his mother's shoulder. Although the child does not relate by seeing, he still sees. Milk is seeping from his mouth. Mother is calm and positive. Mother and child are united by sounds. They can "talk", exchanging sounds as they exchange

milk. After feeding on the intact nipple, the sounds are soft and caressing.

When the time comes to feed at the other breast the child bends back his head and neck, directs his mouth and sucks, but this time he is calm and tender, showing consideration for the cracked nipple. After eating, the child hiccups and burps, perhaps getting rid of the bad milk from the tender breast. After a while he looks around, but is scarcely able to hold up his head and it bobbles.

There seems to be a differentiation in the child's manner of feeding from the two breasts. While the child does not appear to notice (8/2), both Mother and observer are clearly aware of the difference. For example the observer accidentally spoke of blood—instead of milk—flowing from the painful breast.

And in the following, psychic pain in the form of rage or anger is transformed into bodily expressions like screams and then back into psychic acceptance through a physical pain in the child's gums.

May 4, 1994. Conflict, anger, sorrow

The child has frequently been discontented, but mostly this can be immediately dealt with, frequently with a dummy. Sometimes, however, this does not work and the child displays pure anger or rage. He appears completely absorbed in this and the mother cannot do anything that does not further stimulate his rage.

During my observation the mother started the incident by whipping cream with an electric beater. She was doing this when I entered and my presence gave the child the opportunity of attracting his mother's attention. The mother was in a state of discontent or frustration and the child was sitting in a chair staring into space. I took over from the mother, giving them both a chance to act out their irritation. After the cake had been completed according to instructions reaching me over the screams of the child, we went into the sitting room and the mother assumed what appeared to be a kind of semi-depressive position as the child continued to cry violently. The mother seemed to sink deeper into her attitude the more violent the crying became.

The turning point came when the mother put her finger into the child's mouth. Neither the dummy, caresses, or even nursing had previously been able to soothe him, but the bony finger massaging the sore gums overcame the child's pain and enabled him to forget it. Shortly afterwards it was as though the pain was immersed and transformed in the long, deep look they exchanged.

The shudder that arises at this later point, when it is time for the baby to drink, displays a transformation from desire to physical activity.

May 26, 1994

> The differentiation between the two breasts continues as the child grows older, but by now, the child appears to be very interested in taking in new things in any way he can. For example, a glass of sugar-water makes him quiver with excitement.

The looks and the reverie[5] they hold are expressions of the workings of the alpha function.[6]

The mother-child relationship can be considered a model of the relationship between the analyst and the analysand. Both need each other in order to develop and become what they need to be. Hence the concept of the unconscious is a metaphor of the shared consciousness they use to communicate and that neither child nor analysand can contact unaided. The mother or analyst becomes a transmitter, channelling the messages of the unconscious. It is this channel which Bion terms the alpha function and its signals are alpha elements contained alternately by the two consciousnesses.

Definitions

The first determination on the horizontal axis is termed "Definitory Hypotheses" and consists of boxes for gathering sensory impressions, arising in certain ways under certain conditions in "constant conjunctions". For instance, in the definition of, say, "cat" we find fur, character, motor skills and behaviours grouped in certain ways. However, this definition does not encompass meaning or feeling. Hypothetical definitions denote "selected facts". This is primitive, but entirely necessary action, stemming from a belief in the ability of sensory impressions to gather and form stable, lasting impressions that can be names. We must assume that normal neurotic consciousness contains such a capacity for faith, unlike psychotic consciousness, which appears unable to perform those primary mentalization, which are a consequence of establishing selected facts through acts of faith. In therapy, analysts wait for such facts to appear in order to be able to verbalize them through various types of interpretations at their disposal, acquired through analytic training. This very ability to give up memory and desire thus make it possible for faith to appear in its true form—as a creative state of consciousness.

Psi

The following row, named for the Greek letter psi, the initial letter of the word psyche, is often referred to as the lie. This is where perceived reality is modified in order to create a form of protection from unwanted emotions or from insight and growth. This is where that state which classical theory would term defence or resistance is described. Intense, focused attention on aspects of external reality in the form of, e.g., hypostases, projective identifications, etc., deflects attention and consciousness from internal reality. Since internal reality is primary in relation to external reality, this means that external reality is distorted, which is precisely what happens in the case of strong defence mechanisms. One might say that if a person can stand to give up external reality and focus attention on internal reality, it becomes possible for new aspects of reality to come to light during a shift in attention. The pre-conceptions of consciousness may encounter reality and become saturated by it in order to form concepts. The same relations apply between external and internal reality, as between pre-conceptions and saturated concepts that approach the significance of pre-concepts. Thus these are the same relations as exist between phenomena and Plato's ideas, if these ideas are understood as a kind of pre-conceptions; these pre-conceptions are a kind of inborn ideas. In the dialogue *Meno*, Plato demonstrates that the rule of Pythagoras is an innate idea in the consciousness or psychic space of Meno's slave. Meno himself discovers the structure of space and the derived functions hereof expressed by the rule of Pythagoras through Socrates' maieutic method, a kind of therapy. Hence this mathematical rule provides the external, phenomenological world with a mental form as well as a theoretical structure.[7]

Socrates' therapy, Meno's consciousness and the dialogue *Meno* itself, all contain so-called innate ideas, pre-conceptions and Plato's ideas. These are then again contained in the rule of Pythagoras, which contains—or serves as an abstraction for—the source of insight. The key question then, is whether these abstractions actually do approximately contain external reality, thus preventing our mental representations from creating distortion and thereby negative growth. This is what the Sphinx does to Corinth and what Oedipus sensibly seeks but is unable to change.[8]

The psi-column contains those concepts that fixedly and inattentively maintain reality in forms that may no longer be useful. Perhaps the most accessible examples of psi-character belief-systems in the process of becoming inexpedient are found in the sciences when a paradigm shift is underway. For instance, for many years after Galileo, the Aristotelians maintained the notion that bodies fall due to an inner urge for their origins in the ground. This urge was supposedly greater for stones than for feathers. We sometimes see it in politics where politicians cannot give up their viewpoints and are overtaken. Thus old doctrines have psi character relative to new ones, although the question of which is more approximate to the truth is an entirely different story.

Notation, attention, "Oedipus" (Inquiry)

In the following columns the actions express increasing degrees of cooperation and each column may be subdivided a number of times. Thus many different forms of notation may be created to support many different kinds of memory (notes, tape-recordings, films, witnesses, etc.). There are a number of ways to be attentive or listen, just as the column termed inquiry contains numerous methods (sensing, statistic operationalisation, measurements, etc.). This column was originally called Oedipus in reference to the forms of investigation outlined in the drama by Sophocles. Naturally this column can also contain methods that are only peripherally indicated by Sophocles, or not mentioned at all, since they were not discovered or developed at the time.

Actions

The last row of action includes both actions that take place after a careful working through of the entire mental apparatus and those denoted projective identification, introjection, incorporation, and acting out. These types of actions are clearly observable in the previous excerpts from infant observation reports.

2. The vertical axis, beta elements and pre-conceptions

The vertical axis lists different categories of statements. Thus there is a distinction between degrees of abstraction and generalization and thereby between various forms of ontological status. This may also be expressed by pointing out that this axis seeks to catalogue the contents of psychic space by dividing it into sections of increasing abstraction. Beta elements are at the most concrete end of the scale with algebraic calculus at the most abstract, although its form or character and usefulness vis-à-vis psychic space has yet to be discovered.

When Bion was working with individuals in group therapy before and during World War II, he discovered that groups had a tendency to function at a more primitive level than did individuals. Individual decisions were characterized by symbols, thought, assessments and choice. He coined the term "basic assumption mentality" to describe the more primitive functioning of groups (Bion, 1961). He believed that the psychic processes of this mentality expressed more or less what Freud termed primary processes, originating from deep-rooted, unconscious layers of consciousness that Bion termed the protomental apparatus. At this level ego was not distinct from the body, rather ego and body were one. This means that physical states do not obtain mental representation and hence that emotional experiences are construed as bodily states to which the body immediately reacts with other bodily states and actions. These emotional experiences then exist as internal and external sensory data or bodily states and these are what Bion terms beta elements. When they are transformed through what Bion term the alpha function, they become alpha elements, which may then be organized in symbols, and structured and ordered into dream thoughts that can become thought in the wakeful state. However, there are a number of beta elements that are not transformed, and which can neither be remembered nor processed, but which may be evacuated or stored in the body, where they may become various forms of compulsive behaviours like phobias, tics, tensions or motor disorders. They may appear in dreams, fantasies or hallucinations as bizarre elements and perhaps they can even create disturbances at the cellular level or become psychotic, neurotic, or otherwise defensive actions or thoughts. Perhaps these stores of beta elements form the basis of somatic conditions and of what Winnicott terms the "false self". The main thing is that when these conditions are active, thinking ceases at the symbolic level. Hence these are also the conditions that dominate when we regress into various forms of group mentality, where we give up on making sense of our emotional experiences. The Danish cartoon crisis demonstrates this level clearly in both Danes and Muslims. This group-mentality level is otherwise best known in youth gangs, national socialist groups or various terrorist organizations. However, regression or what may be referred to as consciouslessness also exists in every institution as an instrument for securing the rights of this particular group. This is a well-known phenomenon in groups of doctors, psychologists and semi-skilled workers.

In his *Brazilian Lectures,* Bion explains that beta elements are used to discuss things non-verbally, without thinking about them. A blushing man or woman tells a long story. This narrative expresses beta elements without being them and the story is alpha elements without being them. This situation lies between the proto-mental apparatus, which is entirely beyond communication, and the mental apparatus that uses various forms of verbal communication.

Perhaps this is the level of speech imagined by Wittgenstein in his enigmatic statement that "whereof one cannot speak, thereof one must be silent" (Wittgenstein, 1922). The statement is a marker of the border into that space where the creation of meaning and the meaningful are developed. This may also be the border Plato indicates with his statement that no serious person ever expresses serious things in writing (Johansen 1991, p. 5). His cave-image might be an attempt to illustrate a similar connection, where the world of ideas is *prior* to the proto-mental apparatus; the shadows on the wall of the cave are the determinations of what ideas we can sense and the stone wall itself is the proto-mental apparatus. (Beta screen)

The chained people are then an image of that part of consciousness which is active, while the one person who is free to move into the light to behold the ideas is an image of our possibilities of reaching truth and becoming one with reality. That is to say an image of consciousness identical to itself.

As adults we may experience or see how beta elements arise, when we carefully study babies in nursing situations. We assume that a nursing baby can experience envy (Klein, 1959, p. 176)[9] vis-à-vis the strength, love, warm superiority and security streaming from the mother to the baby both as milk, maternal love, security and wisdom. This envy can make the baby attack the breast in rage, creating a conflict within the infant between the need to nurse to survive and the fear of retribution from the recently-attacked breast. Bion says that envy and aggression can ruin a normal relationship between the infant and the breast. The baby is strung out between murderous and suicidal emotions on one hand, and feelings of love, security and well-being, on the other. But the baby is unable to distinguish between these feelings, the breast, milk, and internal and external stimuli arising in and around the nursing situation. In other words, the baby is unable to distinguish between the physical and the psychic, since it has yet to establish an alpha function to do this job. Instead, the baby "splits" the ambivalent emotions and sensory impressions, projecting that which is unbearable and perhaps idealising that which feels good. This gives rise to confusion concerning the significance of a need for material and psychic experiences or sensing and emotion—or perhaps more specifically yet: milk and love.[10]

However, there are many obvious examples of this confusion continuing into adulthood in the various forms of greed for objects or sex so omnipresent in our culture. The beta elements present, that might be responsible for these states, whether we term them imbalances, perversion, disease or normality, are—according to this line of though—bodily frustrations of need seeking satisfaction through frustrated, hopeless, acquisitive activities with silly investments, collecting-manias, Scrooge-like behaviour, various abusive relationships involving food, drugs, power, sound, and work, etc. Our so-called welfare-model or our western culture is awash with examples.

> When the child is to be weaned, the mother has more solid food on hand, so the child will not perish. Fortunate the one who has this stronger nourishment handy! (Kierkegaard, 2006, p. 11)

For Kierkegaard, this stronger nourishment is faith, as it is with Bion. He sees the infant's opportunity for growth and survival in the act of faith and love constituted by the use of the alpha function on sensory impressions, feelings and emotions. He sees this happening in the mother's reverie. Only through such actions can we speak of psychic development, where pre-conceptions and perhaps beta elements as well are transformed into building blocks for the psyche or into alpha elements. These transformations then lead to change and perhaps to psychic growth. This can also happen in therapy through the free-flowing attention of the therapist without memory or desire, in the moments constituted by the meetings between analyst and analysand.

3. Alpha elements, alpha function, reverie or meditation

The transition from beta elements and pre-conceptions to alpha elements and more advanced building blocks of the psyche always takes place through relations and the alpha function or reverie. Bion claimed that psychoanalysis is the work that takes place in the clinic between the analyst and the analysand and that this work is where analysts utilize their alpha functions and their reverie (Grinberg, 1990).

This is because Bion believed that psychoanalysis constitutes a development that may be understood as a search for truth and that this search for truth could only take place through the experiences or transformations arising when a meeting takes place between an I and a you, where both are dissolved in a state of no memory, no desire, free-flowing attention or reverie, thereby touching "O". Any form of search or creation takes place in polarity, of which the simplest is that duality which is precisely what is expressed in the psychoanalytic meeting between analyst and analysand. Heraclitus expressed this same insight in his claim that all is strife (Kirk & Raven, 1971).[11]

Hence what Bion is dealing with is the activity that takes place through transformations towards growth or creativity. Creativity or growth are themselves incomprehensible and are perhaps acts of God, since humans are not even capable of creating a single leaf.

Bion envisages this creativity as the human thought apparatus capturing thoughts that "are" in this "O" and processing them. He terms the working process the alpha function. This alpha function which is capable of seizing thoughts is also capable of seizing bodily expressions, internal and external stimuli, or beta elements, which it can then transform into alpha elements intended for further use by the thought apparatus. This work gives rise to preconceptions and then moves on down the vertical axis, concepts or thought systems in the form of myth, theory, calculations, etc. We must also assume that these forms of thought are perceived as being identical with our thought apparatus. When I for instance manipulate myths as I try to do in the chapter b on myth as a model for growth. We have an expression of a thought apparatus. The thought apparatus is stored in our memory and on the bookshelves at the library. It is destroyed by auto-da-fés and through attacks on the alpha function that may, for instance, take place through envy. It puts us to sleep during sessions and during class; time and time again we come to resemble Palinurus, desperately holding onto our tools of control in the form of scientific theory or perhaps outdated "common sense" observations (Vergil, 1994–2000, Book Five, lines 827–870).

Perhaps this is the same creativity that is displayed in the myth of the Virgin Birth, where Christ—the harbinger of the new—emerges from that same, formless, infinite void termed God the father or "O". The first verse of the Gospel of John may perhaps express the same theory as Bion:

> In the beginning was the Word, and the Word was with God, and the Word was God. The same was in the beginning with God. All things were made by Him, and without Him was not anything made that was made. (John 1:1–3, 21st Century King James Version)

I think it is possible to illuminate this creative function by schematizing the dyadic relationships into three models of relating that express both internal and external object-relations. When speaking of internal object-relations, the models also describe a state of consciousness that may dominate the relationships arising for this person in their surroundings: mutual, symbiotic and parasitic relations (Bion, 1970).

Bion attempts a kind of mathematical model in his search to describe these meetings. The mutual meeting is denoted O̲, where the line and the O touch each other at one single point as a tangent. This sign may either express confusion, obscurity or diffuse togetherness during therapy. The working relation continues and the meeting has been partly unregarded, but may yet have been active. Ø expresses symbiotic relations and may denote the relation between symbol and symbolized reality or fantasy, be it conscious or unconscious. O̲ where there is no contact between O̲ and the line is the parasitic relation, dominated by projective counter-identifications or certain projective identifications. There is no actual contact between the analyst and the analysand—since one or both—is dominated by the psychotic part of their personality (Grinberg, 1990).

Actual creativity takes place only in the symbiotic meeting. I shall attempt to illustrate the nature of these meetings in the following clinical material.

1. Mutual (commensal) relations, where two people share a third object to the benefit of all

One example might be two rowers in a double sculler and their relation to the boat, when there is balance and thrust in the boat. This mutual relation may be an intellectual or mental activity unfolded in a community, where all other relations between the individuals are inconsequential. An ideally functioning supervisory relation can be an expression of this relation too. It may also be a legally regulated relationship like certain noble marriages of the Renaissance or between business partners.

One side of therapeutic relations should be mutual, the agreement: the client comes (and pays). The therapist is present (and accepts payment). The shared third and unknown object then becomes therapy.

2. Symbiotic relations, where two people share a common feeling or a common object

The nature of these relations is essentially indescribable outside mysticism, for how can two be one? Nevertheless, this kind of union is a fact symbolically described, e.g., in the unifying Christian metaphysics surrounding the Eucharist, in Buddhist metaphysics concerning the Samantabhadra/Samantabhadri, and in the alchemic or Jungian metaphysics concerning a creative *coniunctio*. In clinical meetings this relation must be understood as a meeting between two consciousnesses that become one to later separate again. This meeting is the decisive vortex of the therapeutic process. It takes place, when this process is to be instigated and it can take place within each individual therapeutic session. When this happens there an effect will spread like rings in the water or like a pressure wave in the ocean of consciousness and in the social field in and around therapy.

In Christian dogma, the mystery of the Holy Trinity is a metaphoric expression of the same form of insight in a yet more subtle form, since this mysticism includes a precise metaphor for "O" in the form of the Holy Spirit or the dove, floating down to impregnate consciousness or, more specifically, the womb of Mary, permitting creation and the ensuing growth of the foetus to take place. The Oedipus myth also touches on the mystery of creativity with its dynamic of destruction/creation described in the triangular mother-father-child relation.[12]

3. Parasitic relations, where two people share a third object, but all are destructive to one another

This relation appears most obviously in therapeutic settings when the parties involved do not think. Their ability to think has been destroyed. The object around which a mutual and symbiotic partnership exists is thinking, which is destroyed. The fact that there is no thought is known from a series of group processes, where individuals function in a form of regressed modus and where unconscious and highly emotionally charged psychic matter is expressed. This is a phenomenon we see in large group processes. We also see it in therapy, when the client uses the therapist as a container for unconscious feelings and matter. The therapist then becomes a "toilet breast" in which the client expunges part of his or her waste. In the case of strongly aggressive, unconscious feelings of the client towards the therapist or towards others, therapists may feel sleepy or depressive as a form of defence against their own potential aggressive or destructive actions. In this sort of parasitic relation, projective identification is a common form of communication. This situation can be illustrated by the unveiled sphinx, plunged into darkness whence it continues to destructively dominate consciousness, creating death, sterility and plague.

The brief example below details a telephone conversation in which a meeting is arranged to initiate a therapeutic process that may be interpreted as an expression of all 3 models. Thus these models are not to be understood as an image of a personality, but as images of the modification of the consciousness of personality. These modifications take place from one second to the next. Consciousness is continuously undergoing modification.

Not all clients benefit from being forced out of the sensory perception of symbiotic relations into an intellectual relation to the analyst. This depends on the client's ability to switch from a predominantly sensory level of functioning in the "here and now" to a largely intellectual level of mutual functioning:

> The friend of a young girl's mother calls on behalf of a young girl to inquire into the possibility of the girl entering therapy. The girl has anorectic problems and is not in touch with her parents. The therapist suggests that the girl calls to make an appointment. After a few days the girl calls. After an in-depth description of her problems, where the therapist is largely in listening mode, an appointment is made. She is given a very detailed description of how to find the clinic, what public transport to use, the location of the bus stop in relation to the clinic, the appearance of the house, etc.
>
> During the conversation the therapist makes a note of the fact that she becomes unusually explanatory, careful and compassionate in her accentuations.
>
> During the telephone conversation, the therapist makes an unusually conscious effort to ask the girl to cancel her appointment if she is prevented from coming.

> After their conversation she wonders whether the young girl will show up and is full of doubt as to whether she will be able to help the girl, not least because the girl expressed doubts as to whether she would be able to make the allotted appointment, was unsure whether she wanted that particular slot, and because the therapist was given to understand that there would be a number of interruptions if a therapeutic process was to be initiated.
>
> The next day the young girl's mother's friend calls, describing how the girl called her after the telephone conversation, crying violently about the condescending treatment she had received.
>
> Two days later the young girl calls to say that she would very much like to come at the allotted time. She forwards a detailed bio prior to the meeting and arrives on schedule, so therapy can begin.

It appears likely that the girl felt it was provocative to be forced into the harsh realities of having to do something as difficult as seeking out, finding, allotting time and committing to resolving her problems. This difficult reality becomes persecutory. The girl has held off from facing these problems, her own weakness and feelings of insufficiency, by perceiving the therapist to be persecutory. She has not been able to contain the therapist listening in empathy while at the same time being specifically demanding with her directions. The therapist's shift from a more specific tone of voice, normal for giving directions, to empathetically sympathetic and understanding is an expression of a vain attempt to hold on to the aspects of the symbiotic meeting that had begun with the empathetic listening of the therapist. Finally the therapist senses the girl's lack of motivation as an expression of therapy already being perceived as persecutory. The relation has become parasitic. The therapist enters defence mode and does not get a chance to think of the changes taking place in herself in the form of her lowered and more empathetic tone of voice in order to use it to understand the girl.

The therapist feels persecuted and seeks to guard herself against being stood up by emphasizing the need to cancel appointments. The therapist feels persecuted precisely because symbiotic meetings with their empathy provide a good opportunity for projective identification to arise and in this case the projective identification is destructive, thus rendering the relation parasitic.

In interpreting the above example the transference creating the dyadic relationships is understood as being of a more sensuous nature, where the two share a feeling, leaving no borders between them, nor two separate internal spaces. The therapist's decision *to* interpret breaks this sensuous transference, and the transference become intellectual in nature through this choice, when the therapist formulates her interpretation or offers her explanation. This increases the girl's anxiety and her defences are activated as an attack on the connection that we have termed intellectual, where there are two separate spaces: The girl speaks of interruption etc. Thus the girl expresses an unconscious desire to recreate unity. This then happens in the girl's imagination and is staged through her letter writing to the therapist once a form of de-toxification has taken place in "surrendering" the tears and anger to her mother's friend.

The mutual relation is expressed in the fact of the girl's writing and showing up on schedule. The client feels that she and the therapist have a shared assignment on which to work. The client writes and shows up and the therapist is present and receives her payment. Meltzer perceives this mutual relation as that which is formed between the client and the inner, psychic adult object representations of the therapist (Meltzer, 1970).[13]

This merged relation appears in the client's empathetic meeting with the therapist, who is understanding and consoling as the client is understood and consoled (container-contained). It is expressed partly through the girl's confidences and partly through the change in the tone of voice of the therapist. The ambition is to maintain the identification that has been created. On the basis of this relation they agree to meet.

Meanwhile, this is precisely where the symbiotic relation leads to a sort of "mutative" leap, since the empathetic form of communication is transformed into an intellectual form of communication when the analyst is obliged to give directions. The symbiosis mounts an anxious defence. This is projected from the client into the analyst, who also becomes anxious about being stood up and reacts by defending herself from this "abuse". The projection is caused by the fact that the client cannot stand the analyst's "abuse" consisting of the analyst "dropping" the client from the empathetic/symbiotic "space". What is created here exemplifies a parasitic relation—in the form of the "abuse" i.e., the "dropping".

There is a mutual destruction, disabling the analyst's ability to think, causing the adult part of the client to break down, as well as the destruction of the space in which therapy is to take place.

In this case therapy was instigated nonetheless due to a basic trust or confidence that exists in a shared psychic space: one space, one faith and one confidence, shared by both.

4. The alpha function

These creative processes of consciousness discovered by Bion precede that part of the psyche discussed by Freud and termed the primary processes. These in turn precede the forms of thought Jung refers to as symbolic in *Symbols of Transformation* (1956) as well as what Klein terms unconscious fantasy, although this organizational level is what comes closest to these creative processes. This "Bionic" part of the psyche is devoid of mental or symbolic representation. It has no judgmental or decisive functions and perceives only states of belonging: inside-outside, for-against. Furthermore, there is only a "body ego" and hence everything is a bodily state or action. Beta elements and the so-called alpha function also belong in this area.[14] In the following we shall term these beta elements sensory data where "sensory" relates to the material and "data" to the mental part of consciousness.[15] Assisted by Meltzer and Bion we shall term the "place" where these creative processes take place the proto-mental part of consciousness.

Alpha function failure

Sensory material can be transformed into mental material through what Bion terms the alpha function, although we do not know how this happens, only that it does (Bion 1970, pp. 11–12). However, we also know that it sometimes fails. When this is the case the unconscious sensory input becomes waste residue in the body or the psyche. This waste is termed beta elements, and is—as I understand it—a cross between mental and material representations. The nature of this waste of the psyche or consciousness can vary depending on the emotions involved; the bodily version of this waste can become somatisations.

Body and psyche have at least three different ways of handling this pollution.

One way can be to regress into a kind of pre-mental mode of functioning, which is what happens, e.g., in group- and mass-phenomena and frequently in the case of extreme collective violence (large-group mentality, fascism, racism, cultural ethnicism, good/bad, paranoid-, schizoid thought, etc.).[16]

Another can be through different kinds of somatisation in the form of eating disorders, sexual perversions, tics (e.g., Tourette syndrome), or rigid body posture, body language, etc.). The aetiology of most of our known diseases is quite uncertain.

A third, more common, way is through feelings of meaninglessness or emptiness, or through hallucinatory or diffuse thinking (manic and grandiose defences, etc.).

In cases of severe schizoid and narcissistic disorders, consciousness is maintained at a pre-mental level, where splitting is the dominant form. Various forms of projective identification are the dominant form of communication. Similarly violence may be the only possible means of communication. The violence then purges or detoxifies the mind of its pollution.

One could say that those who release unbearable emotionality in the first two ways avoid the difficult processing of these emotions in the third pollutant form; that processing, however, is what is most likely to lead to a development of the mental apparatus.

Emotional processing takes place throughout life from conception to death in all three ways in our relations to other people: mother, father, siblings, friends, enemies, colleagues, lovers. It takes place in dyads, triads, and groups as well as in therapy. The fora or consciousness modifications where processing takes place are the aforementioned three typical relational forms between external or internal objects: the mutual, the symbiotic and the parasitic.

Working alpha function

We do not know how sense or sensory data (beta elements) achieve mental status or become alpha elements. All we know is that this happens through an unknown process, which Bion terms the alpha function.

A working alpha function is a prerequisite for moving from the paranoid/schizoid position to the depressive position. When this is not the case, movement takes place in the direction of the paranoid-schizoid. Consciousness is always flowing in one direction or another, since we are either moving towards the paranoid-schizoid or a depressive pole.

The alpha function is specifically human. When it is working perfectly it transforms all sensory data into mental representations. If this does not happen these untransformed sensory data are stored as a kind of pollution of the psyche.[17]

The experience of any form of pollution can lead to a desire for detox or therapy.[18] Therapeutic meetings create a kind of "field" where all previous experiences can be processed. This field is felt when the intensity of the therapeutic meeting is discovered, and is the "here and now" where transference takes place. Thus the field is in a way the "atmosphere" or quality inherent in the meeting or individual session. Beta elements can be ejected into this "field" and deflected. "The Field" is created and maintained by "tools" possessed by therapists. These are above all the therapists' container/contained function, their alpha function—i.e., their ability to transform sensory material into mental representations through "thinking" or "dreaming",[19] as well as their capacity for "reverie" or "free-floating attention". The objective is primarily to create a greater degree of freedom and mobility of consciousness, thus making the movement of the psyche tend towards the depressive position.

This "tension" that has been termed the analysts' neutrality, but which might equally be referred to as their ability for compassion, love and empathy; or perhaps "free-floating attention" or "no-memory and no desire" function might also be a way of describing this field (Lambert, 1981).[20]

The transitions from the paranoid/schizoid position to the depressive unfold the emotions and the "tensions" between the client and the therapist, of which they may be aware and which they may be able to put into words.

Ideally the therapists' emotions are their very particular form of attention, which is simultaneously clear and a form of reverie, which aims equally "outwards" in an empathic feeling for the client and "inwards" in a sensing of oneself. It is also a kind of neutral observation that listens without hearing anything in particular, is without doing, knows without knowledge, and sees without judging. This field is the only place where beta elements may surface.

In other words therapy then becomes the place where sensing and emotional experiences are staged as transference and verbalized as transformations.

Bion perceives dreams as an expression of initial symbolizations. Dreams are thus a result of the work of the alpha function. A person's dreams are a short-cut to the understanding and processing of emotional experiences, which the wakeful or conscious mental apparatus of the person in question has not been able to reach, perhaps because he or she is still insufficiently familiar with the ability for inner reflection or unable to utilize the alpha function effectively enough. One might say that dreams have done a part of the work of translating beta elements from the proto-mental apparatus. Thus emotions may be lifted from dreams into mental space, gaining room through narratives. This may happen when what is recalled turns into "memory"[21]—using the terms as Bion would—during the conversation on the dream and its associations.

Thus Bion sees no principal distinction between insights obtained in dreams, thought, poetry, myth or science. Except perhaps that good scientific insights have the advantage of being quickly disproved.

The alpha function is most precisely defined through its mode of functioning. This may be because it has a kind of axiomatic status that cannot be justified but only demonstrated by its consequences.

In the following brief example I shall try to demonstrate how the alpha function appears to work within an established therapeutic situation. This also means that I shall try to show how consciousness moves towards the depressive position.

First example:

(a) **I say:** but there is something magnificent about those mighty feelings in that black hole.
Q says: Perhaps I've organized my life around living it in those emotions.
Perhaps, I say, this is what we referred to as "home-liness".
Q says: I am staging it myself, like the other day when I told

you about masturbating next to .... That was the terrible thing ... ((telling about it)).

(b) **I say,** yes, but nothing happened. Perhaps this terrible thing isn't so terrible after all.
Q: It's hard to give up the incredible, special and home-ly aspects of it.
I say: Yes, maybe we want to be special and it can be hard to discover that you are just an ordinary man with a bit of domestic trouble that is probably even temporary.
Q says in the end, that it seems to be a question of becoming convinced that there is nothing to be afraid of. Like the weather, this too shall pass; even the fact of being seized by a fear of becoming psychotic is a state that will eventually pass.

(c) **I say:** I would like to put words to what you are describing.
Q gives me a questioning look.
I say: Merriness.[22]
Q looks pleased: Yes, that's it. Q continues: The Dalai Lama is like that.
Q speaks of this being a form of naïveté, but then the Dalai Lama is not naïve.
I refer to St. Paul's injunction to "Pray without ceasing. In every thing give thanks".[23] Paul was neither naïve nor banal.
I say: Now you've been in this state for the last few minutes and nothing has happened.
Q looks a little surprised and happy. He says: Of course merriness is wonderful; after all this is the creativity of life itself.[24]

The alpha function appears to play out in three phases:

During the first phase a form of tension takes place within the psyche, since the shame, the powerlessness and the humiliation as well as the anger and the hopelessness of a real or imagined rejection related to the situation of masturbating behind his wife's back in the marital bed are remembered. This psychic tension is the equivalent of the bodily tension related to masturbation and this tension can be processed since it can be contained in the trusting relationships developed between client and analyst. This tension is an expression of a grandiose victimhood or a kind of masochistic enjoyment.

During the second phase, this tension is digested, understood and normalized. It is understood as a common human state. The tension is relaxed and a form of psychic ejaculation takes place into the mind of the therapist. What could not be achieved through masturbation appears to be successful in therapy.

However, the mental release does not take place until phase c—through understanding of and symbolisation and association with a large part of Q's psyche, including his feelings of abandonment, betrayal, loneliness, smallness, insufficiency and inferiority—when the situation is labelled with the word 'merriness'.

Perhaps the release becomes evident by being associated with spiritual figures such as the Apostle Paul and the Dalai Lama.

The term "merriness" has become significant—in the "private therapeutic language" we have constructed—of the state that Q has discovered within himself, hidden behind a masochistic or self-destructive defence acquired as a way of adapting to *a feeling of the world* surrounding Q during childhood. The term destroys or poisons joy through its derisive, derogatory connotations.

Apparently Q accepts that it is possible to unite the pain associated with feelings of rejection or inferiority with the joy of creativity and confidence. There is movement towards joy or acceptance arising from the fact that the self with its polarities and ambivalences becomes more unified and whole.

Second example:

> **Q says:** I remember the other day you said something about me taking you in somehow.
> Yes, I say, what was that about?
> **Q says:** but that merriness is a kind of humorous attitude to inferiority, about inability and trying against the odds while accepting the inevitability of sometime failure.
> Precisely, I say.
> I mention the inner fool and we discuss the relationship between the fool and his master.
> **Q says:** But they are in opposition (talking about the fool and the master)
> **I say:** Yes, but that is precisely why they love each other. They also know that they cannot do without each other. They are connected.
> Q says that they can count on one another, they trust each other, so they can do anything and yet they need each other as opposites.[25]

I am under the impression that the above example is an illustration of the alpha function and the way it moves consciousness towards acceptance of the possible polarity of existence. We understand or feel from the inside that this duality is not necessarily animosity or war.[26] These maximum differences can also be mutually fruitful and enriching. The alpha function enables the motion from either-or towards a win-win situation. Once this has been acknowledged, both good and bad can be met with trust and anticipation. Consciousness moves from a mainly destructive modification leading to negative growth to another modification that is mainly creative and leads to positive growth.

One might say that Bion somehow focuses on the thought processes that take place both during dreaming and wakefulness. He dissects them and terms their smallest constituent part, "thing-in-itself" or "idea"; eternal, unchangeable and untouchable, it becomes that ephemeral substance we call thought, "knowing", alpha element, or beta element. "Being" is the here-and-now—a creativity at once material, chemical, psychic and energetic. This "is" is understood or mentalised as a modification "in" consciousness.

One might continue to say that Bion describes how sensory data are transformed into psychic data, which are turned into mythic images or obtain dream status. The ability to dream and to wake is our tool. This ability constitutes the binocularity with which we "see" and gain insight. Dreams are the "reversible perspective" of wakefulness and vice versa. Thus we organize our data by setting them aside. We turn them into dream data, mythologizing them, and observe others as wakeful-state data.

This movement is going on around the clock in a certain rhythm. It takes place through a shift between different levels of attention and by the cognitive activities that Kant describes in *The Critique of Pure Reason*. In this work it would appear that perception is almost like Bion's "conceptions" while apperception is the formless, infinite void or "O". Thus pre-conceptions—like alpha elements—are intermediate stages, while the alpha function is the name of the unknown force translating or connecting apperception and perception.

Psychic data are invented or discovered by the foetus or the baby through the registration of pain, desire and disgust. Hence all psychic data are polluted or coloured by these categories. A concept or a word is thus always a container for elements of desire/disgust/pain and therefore—like all life—in constant movement. Understanding is a kind of grasping mother's hand for security, or like reaching for mother with some other body part; the eyes, mouth or nose. However, the baby may let the mother go and come, can release and catch, can look and look away, and can even do so physically/sensorily as well as imaginarily as a psychic object. Thus the baby achieves stable development. This training is constantly ongoing in play as well as in all other activities, such as peek-a-boo games, sleeping-waking, going-coming, waving, playing hide-and-seek, sand play, the dinner table, in bed, on the changing table, etc.

Many of these exercises—which are basically about losing and regaining—seem to repeat in therapy, such as separating and meeting on either side of weekends, for instance, or holidays. The separation problematic is also formulated in a mild form in the separation after therapy to meet at the following session and perhaps generally in all sorts of absences including delays, no-shows and postponements. Growth arises in recognitions and working with them.

This enormous journey—undertaken by the foetus or the baby from the thing-in-itself to dream thoughts, concept-formation etc., by means ranging from distortion (psi) over notation, attention etc., to action—requires space. A journey requires space. This space is peopled with a self, a kind of thought-producing condensate, and an inner mother, who helps process these thoughts. The baby has a content contained by the mother. Together they are a thinking couple that the baby can internalize in its space as a model.

The mother receives the cries of the child and gives them back to the baby in a thoroughly processed form through her different responses, which the baby can then schematize. This is also what takes place in therapy. It is as though the monochromatic cries of the baby break into crystals and are thrown back in an orgy of colour for the child to arrange in hierarchies. This work goes on when the baby endures the frustration that arises when its needs are not immediately met. While this frustration is being endured, what is happening is that the baby's innate pre-conceptions meet the alpha elements that the mother has made from the beta elements expressed in the child's screams and other gestures, and subsequently projected into the mother as beta elements, which are then returned to the child in alpha element form.

Of course these words can seem irritating and be seen as one unknown replacing another, which is true enough. However there is probably no great difference between the feeling concerning this and of the feeling around concepts like particles, protons, neutron, photons, quarks etc., apart—perhaps—from the fact that the training we have all undergone in school etc., enables us to see these constructions as a more secure finger for our baby hand to seize than a mere feeling.

Melanie Klein generalizes Freud's theory of instincts in that she sees foetus and baby as defined by a need to relate; initially to the breast and subsequently to entire individuals. The individual is communicative and inclined to insight. Bion underpins this since he holds the opinion that the baby is also trying to obtain contact with, relate to and gain insight into him- or herself. The child uses the mother as a helper in this primary process. Her opinion and later all "second opinion" is a vehicle for growth. This condensate of innate and acquired pre-conceptions, saturated and unsaturated concepts constitute the self and the individual unconscious. Bion does not perceive the unconscious as composed of instinctual forces or as id mixed with phylogenetic sediments like the Oedipus complex, but rather as thoughts or pre-conceptions.

Thus Bion's perception of the unconscious is far closer to Jung's since both consider the unconscious a kind of infinite cosmic void, with an infinite number of possible contents or potential materializations. Bion presumes that the baby has a kind of innate depressive position with an all-containing cosmic unified consciousness. Jung sees the baby symbol as an expression of the same; of "becoming" or of ultimate creativity. Jungian psychology can also be understood as an attempt at generalizing Freud's theory of instincts by adding other transcendental structures in the psyche through archetypal theory. At conception and again at birth, reality interferes violently with psychic space, which through its pre-conceptions and thoughts encompasses a kind of ultimate potential for attention. This is the space the mystic Bion discovers, and which is described with the Ps<=>D metaphor. Perhaps this is also what Freud senses in expressing the opinion that there is a greater likeness between intra-and extra-uterine life than one would initially assume.

The resistance of the ego then becomes not the struggle against id or instinct, but the battle towards an understanding of the meaning of instinct or towards "a preconceptive marriage with their realizations" (Grotstein, 1990). Unsaturated pre-conceptions are saturated, when thoughts find a thinker the thinker thinks the thoughts.

Thus Bion's interpretation of divine wrath over the fruits of insight as the basic expression of the myth of original sin, the Oedipus myth and the myth of the Tower of Babel is elucidated. Anger is aimed at the understanding of life's very imprisonment in reality; the blindness of the self in the form of the paranoid-schizoid states in which it is imprisoned; anger at the lack of freedom in spite of freedom and happiness as an omnipresent possibility.

The sphinx of the Oedipus myth expresses this dilemma, for the sphinx is and has the riddle and its solution means that the sphinx is thrown into infinite darkness. Knowledge of *who* we are entails a darkness where we forget phenomena, ideas, concepts, knowledge, theories, dreams, etc., forget that we are. Thus we arrive at "being". We give up "knowledge of". This may be the journey described by St. John of the Cross as the dark night of the soul (Bion 1984, pp. 147–149, 158).

Thus Bion's interpretation becomes reminiscent of gnosis, alchemy and other mystic thought.

However, if we consider this thinking in a more technical perspective, its significance is extensive: the paranoid-schizoid state is necessary to activate thinking. This is what happens through negative transference, with frustration and acting out in therapy. It also happens in positive transference, through humour and various forms of identifications. When changes have taken place, loneliness is increased along with the ability to endure the depressive position, where empathy and the longing for truth may be the only energy that can spur us on.

b. Myth as a model for growth: Oedipus Rex and Oedipus at Colonos

1. Oedipus Rex

Greek mythology constitutes an extensive attempt to somehow chart that psychic space where creation and creative growth are in focus, just as in the "Grid". Hesiod poses and answers the questions of where we come from, who we are, how we become what we are, in a number of different ways. These are juicy stories full of aggression and sex, couplings, rapes and castrations. Encounters arise primarily between male and female, but it is as though the babies, when they come, are not a result of these meetings and they are not raised by the parents; the encounters are only rarely about love and there are even examples of self-fertilisation. Sex is mainly a question of a penetrative desire for ownership and/or the desire for domination. This applies to both sexes. We usually encounter the offspring as adults, however, the myths do detail the infancy of Zeus, Apollo and Dionysus, but the point is that they are raised away from their fathers and mothers for fear that they will be annihilated by them. The offspring is swallowed by the mother in the shape of Gaia or the father in the form of Chronos.

Naturally these tales reveal the character of the narrating psyche. I understand the myths as a kind of mnemotechnic expression of an era's understanding of its own consciousness. Thus the myths express the relations into which it is possible to enter, as they appear in the space of consciousness and thereby also in external space. They were created at a time where there were vast resources available to those seeking psychic insight or creative growth; material growth was not of much interest to society elite because the satisfaction of material needs within the technical framework available seemed straightforward.

In the era following the achievement of these psychic insights, the physical and material framework collapsed as a consequence of the Peloponnesian war, and the particular cosmopolitan spirit of the Greek city states faced its dissolution. A new so-called Hellenistic space was then able to arise, including what was once perceived to be the whole world. When Freud re-constructed the Oedipus myth in his interpretation as a central model for describing psychic space, there were also violent destructive attacks taking place on the cosmopolitan spirit emanating from Freud's fin-de-siècle Vienna. The old world collapsed through the wars of the 1900s and one might expect a new, quite different, globalised and "neo-Hellenistic" world to rise from the ruins of the old. In ancient Hellenism east met west as will probably turn out to be the case for the "neo-Hellenistic" world of the 21st century.

It is as though increased psychic insight launches formidable attacks against the preservation of these insights through the destruction of the social and societal structures that made possible this encounter with the deeper layers of consciousness.

Perhaps history or reality is a particularly clever version of the myth of the Tower of Babel. If we come to close too consciousness itself, the ur-ground or god, our material and communicative tools splinter.

Perhaps all real creative growth creates its destructive opposite. Or in Bion's terms: Ps<=>D.

We find the earliest acknowledgments of psychic structures and growth potentials where the paranoid-schizoid condition described above is diluted, in the groups that in this day and age are connected with religion, literature, myths, fairy-tales and the like. These fields of knowledge are complimentary to what we primarily cover by the name of science and culture. Now as before, each field includes its own "priesthood", its representatives and elites. Bion terms these groups "the establishment" and describes how decisive social polarity exists between establishment and genius or mystic.

The task of the establishment is to create a space for the insights of the mystic, thereby ensuring growth and avoiding psychic stiffness or death. Bion points out that every age has its geniuses and believes that Freud, Marx and Einstein were among the geniuses of our time. The establishment's task is to integrate their thoughts into the social structures that are prerequisite to the growth of ordinary people, who in turn are the prerequisite for the appearance of new geniuses or mystics. Thus Bion describes the task of the human community as identical to that which was seen as the main task of monasteries in both East and West. The cloistered community Athos in northern Greece thus sees as its main task the creation of meditative communities from whence an enlightened person may rise.

I shall limit myself to using images of the psyche gleaned from the Western cultural sphere, but there are similar, equally precise image from India, Egypt and the Middle East that are presumably related to our images. Particularly the groups surrounding Jung were interested in these images (Kundalini, Bardo Thodol or The Tibetan Book of the Dead) although Jung in his main work, *Mysterium Coniunctionis* (1956), focused his interest on Western image-creation depicting psychic growth.

Presumable thoughts on how to develop the psyche have existed for as long as these images, and hence also thoughts on how psychic change and growth might be ensured to permit humanity to move (to use Klein's terms) from a primitive or schizoid level to a non-primitive or depressive level both at the individual and the collective level. We are engaged in a collective as well as an individual struggle to overcome puberty. These are the requirements and the problems of meeting them that are verbalized in the stories of Oedipus.

Here we have the infant's demand for nurture and care, which are not met. The child is maimed and placed in the wilderness at Cithaeron; it is the fatal consequences hereof that the myth expounds. In a psychic sense this demand is an insistence on care for the new, on a consciousness concerning creation and annihilation. It is the demand for the creative triad of mother, father and child. Oedipus is the story and model of one of many possible failures of this creative trinity. Hegel would characterize the Oedipus myth as a possible reflection perhaps self-reflection concerning synthesis. The mother and father are considered as thesis and antithesis and the baby as synthesis. The triangle remains the model for creativity. The dyads of Hesiod's mythology have been abandoned with all their violence and unconsciousness in a decisive evolutionary step. There is a powerful potential for growth in the attempt to acknowledge this. It is where the psyche awakens to rise with a formidably destructive energy. Still, when Oedipus is abandoned, another set of parents step in who want the boy for what he represents; the colossal potential for growth of the child, whose consequence both specifically and symbolically is to become the king of his own house. He is led to these parents, rescued by a shepherd—later the favoured Christian symbol of Antiquity. Think also of the world of difference between the dream expressed by the Oedipus stories and the dream expressed by the stories of the infant Christ—even including the infanticide in Bethlehem. Oedipus' beginnings are charged with the significance of the beginning of life and the beginning of the psyche: the schizoid-paranoid aspects of the parents, the love of the shepherd, and the developmental ambitions of the foster parents. The myth of Christ is charged with solicitude and gentleness vis-à-vis the new, for the baby both in the story of the birth and the tale of the flight from the schizoid icon represented by the infanticide in Bethlehem. The schizoid has been displaced away from the parents over to the ruler Herod; away from the dominant, parasitic aspects of the couple Iocasta and Laius to the creative and symbiotic loving couple in the form of Mary and Joseph.

However, both tales express the destiny of sons as held back in the maternal in the form of Christ's fate on the cross and in his mother's lap, of Michelangelo's Pietà, and of Oedipus at the crossroads and in his mother's bed.

The psychic image of the Oedipus myth is nuanced in the tragedy *Oedipus at Colonos* written when Sophocles was in his 90s. Here a new image of the psyche is formed, where all the figures produce gestalts of shared human psychic space, differently than in *Oedipus Rex*. Conscious and unconscious material is timelessly woven together into a unity undergoing constant growth. Between the elements constituting the two separate images and between the images as unities there exists a kind of Ps<=>D transformation; a sort of tensile field or reversible perspective. The Oedipus we encounter at Colonos is no longer a restless seeker; eyes gouged out, holding the bloody brooch of his mother, his beloved. This Oedipus is a blind old man, accompanied and led by the daughter and sister who loves him. He meets his cultural foster brother Theseus, who offers him shelter that he may finally be united—in the sacred grove of the Eumenides—with that creative black nothingness for which he has probably always been searching.

Christ also gives himself up at the very end to this infinite creative black void: "My God, My God why hast thou forsaken me .... And Jesus cried again with a loud voice and yielded up his spirit" (Matthew, 27:46 & 50).

2. Myth as a narrative of thought

Bion explains that sometimes analytical problems may be better understood by speaking to the client as though they are being haunted or controlled by a ghost from the past. Young children are haunted and controlled by ghosts from the future. These ghosts are a kind of fact for the personality that adults have the opportunity of exploring through their experience and their ability to manipulate these experiences through thought. These personality facts, both one's own as well as those of others, pose a problem to be processed. This is true of children and adults alike. Oedipus is such a haunted child and person (Bion, 1984; 1999).

In principle, the Oedipus tales show to different ways (A. and B.) in which these personality facts may be manipulated by thinking, and the same two—principally different—methods are used in psychoanalysis. Psychoanalytic therapy matches the Oedipus tales on points C. and D. as described below; both indicating psychic transformation or creative growth. C. is the way it mainly takes place in *Oedipus Rex*, and D. the way it mainly takes place in *Oedipus at Colonos*.

1. The vertex of myth:
   A. Apollonian rational: Examination, conversation, sight;
   B. Dionysian emotional or sensed: smell, touch.

2. The vertex of psychoanalysis:
   C. Both conversation (Apollonian) and action in the form of transferential interpretations, projective identification, interpretation, counselling;
   D. "O". Neither conversation nor transferential love, but empathy or transference in the form of Ø, $\underline{O}$ or contain-contained (♂♀) and growth towards Ps<=>D.

This myth also highlights a number of personality elements that have the characteristics of beta elements or pre-conceptions. Bion speaks of the crossroads-personality. This is a personality we all contain as a function or fact in our mode of thinking, the part of us that is active when we find ourselves at a crossroads, i.e., when we need to make a decision. This might be a decision to act, but it could also be a decision to use a constant conjunction (Bion, 1992)[27] in the form of a definition, a column psi concept or a notation. Thus Bion does not distinguish between the concept "cat" or the concept "crossroads-episode" since he believes that both are either constant conjunctions in the psyche or saturated thoughts that have become structures in consciousness. The defining thing about choice is which impulses or emotions dominate consciousness, determining the telos of the psyche, psychic motivation and nurturing the action and bringing it into existence.

Many personality elements of the cross-roads personality or the malleable psyche may be characterized as follows;

3. Bodily vertex (thing-in-itself, Beta elements, somatisation)
   A. Anxiety;
   B. Flight;
   C. Rage;
   D. Suicide: Iocasta; self-blinding: Oedipus;
   E. Club foot, crippling;
   F. Sphinx (human icon intra-psychically determined by the riddle, extra-psychically by form);
   G. Plague.

4. The vertex of optics of thought or action (symbolizations; alpha elements, rigid structures and other transformations).
   A. Fratri- and filicide (Oedipus vis-à-vis Polynices and Eteocles and these vis-à-vis one another, Cain-Abel, Agamemnon-Iphigenia, Abraham-Isaac, Christ-Judas);
   B. Patricide (both Oedipus and Theseus);
   C. Infanticide in Bethlehem, and prior to the Exodus from Egypt;
   D. Matricide (Orestes-Clytemnestra);
   E. Forms of blindness in Oedipus, Iocasta, Tiresias, the shepherds, foster parents etc.;
   F. Homoeroticism (Laius' pederasty with Chrysippus, Pelops' son); Theseus-Oedipus-common cultic location—Athens as new polis;
   G. Incest or "excessive" maternal/paternal bonding, i.e., "filicide".
   H. Father/sister/daughter love (Oedipus/Antigone/Ismene);
   I. Self-destruction—destruction—schizoid polarity;
   J. Love—unity: father/son, father/daughter, mother/son (the foster mother's offer to Oedipus to return to Corinth and be king as narrated in Euripides' lost *Oedipus*), mother/daughter?
   K. Matriarchy-patriarchy? Procreative responsibility, responsibility/honour/shame of creativity, power.

Bion sees the myth of Oedipus as a useful instrument for memorising psychic problems. It is a kind of catalogue of psychic positions and states that are transformations of psychic eternity, its "O". It is a regrettable mistake to perceive this myth as an expression of theories of cause and effect. The fact that these may be present in the narrative is purely due to the fact that they make it easier to remember the infinite complexity of the whole. This catalogue is so useful precisely because of its great complexity, since this is what makes it difficult to avoid continuously seeing new links and connections everywhere, whereby a locking into "column psi" thinking is prevented.

This myth with its numerous elements and their infinite interpretive potential expresses Freud's idea that thinking provides relief or a reduction of frustration. Thus thinking becomes a way of acting that is principally no different from other ways of acting. Thinking can thus fill out the void between emotion—that appears to be the body's way of acting on its own—and other forms of action. Thinking is activated by emotion in order to process it. When it hurts we act and we think. Sometimes this works the other way round. If we do not transform our pain or emotions by thought work, our actions become dominated by beta elements or perhaps alpha elements and dreams. They become primary thinking or dominated by basic assumption group mentality. This becomes penis-thinking, stomach-thinking or perhaps military/industrial complex thinking at the societal level. Then the weapons speak and all voices fall silent.

The urge for truth is overlain with power-drive, anxiety and envy.

3. Myth as a narrative of power

Therapy is about creating contact within a person with that part of this person's history that nurtures his or her growth. That means creating connections that permit the verbalization of thoughts.

Thus therapy is about overcoming the prohibition formulated by Iocasta: Do not interest yourself in your desire. Do not desire your desire. Forget everything about yourself, give up self reflection. Concentrate on kingship, sire children by me, and enjoy life! Let go of your wish to know the truth. Till the earth and make your money in the sweat of your brow, then I will do my part and bear my children in pain. Eat, drink and be merry. Whether they be kings or idlers, dead or alive, they remain my sons, nailed to me with spikes, enfolded in my arms (Sophocles, *Oedipus*, lines 704 and 774–780. See also Hillman, 1991).

Sophocles' drama challenges the early Greek matriarchy whose form and content we unfortunately know mainly from other sources. Sophocles also interprets the meeting between matter/mater/Gaia and spirit/Uranus and shows how this polarity constellates creativity and destructivity.

Children struggle to get older and when they do they struggle to grow up. Adults too may struggle to make their inner children more adult. But they also struggle to come to terms with the fact that—if all goes well, they will die properly and preferably happy, i.e., first the fathers and mothers, then the sons and daughters. In this struggle therapy may be necessary. We meet our history—Jesus spoke of leaving our father and mother to become one flesh with a spouse. This means leaving and forgiving our parents, for only then can we meet our oppositely sexed position (the feminine or the masculine); only then are we free to also be our "opposite" position and freely connect these positions within ourselves. This also means being able to freely connect to the people we meet *en route*.

Fathers and mothers may make mistakes. Laius did when he demanded his son exposed for fear that his son would kill him. Iocasta did when she gave in to Laius' anxiety and again when she covered up the fact that Oedipus was Laius' killer. She must have known, since she immediately upon Oedipus' arrival sent away the shepherd who was with Laius when he was murdered. She made another mistake in not paying attention to Oedipus' club foot, since she knew that her only son's feet had been maimed. Iocasta consciously avoids the revelation that will create truth and hence growth. She refuses to acknowledge her own mortality.[28] Her goal is to ensure her own immortality by maintaining her own line's possession of Thebes. She ensures the matriarchy since the children issuing from it are doubly descended from Iocasta herself. The association she forms with Oedipus becomes parasitic.

Her child, the young Oedipus, also makes mistakes; he is greedy and drinks himself out of his senses. This is arrogant, superficial and oversimplifying in the understandings and interpretations of the world it produces, thus leading to aggressive, temperamental behaviour.

Anxiety is the overriding sentiment. Nobody but the sage Tiresias believes in life as a common wellspring.

What is so interesting about the different elements of this myth is the interpretation of reality that they express. This corruption of reality—if you will—is expressed in the oracle's prognosis of patricide and matriarchy (incest). These statements are "psi-column" statements, i.e., lies that create reality. The lie arises through a wrongful utilization of the alpha function in that it appears to be dominated by beta elements in the form of envy or anxiety. These elements are activated by the infant Oedipus. I think most people are familiar with such elements being activated when spending time with babies. I also think we as therapists recognize this from our meetings with clients. We discover this when we understand the ways in which we have "acted out" both through outer actions and through interpretations or counter-transference.

One cold winter's day a client steps into the hallway where she deposits her coat. The therapist has just opened the door and is waiting for her to come into the therapy room. This client has been in therapy for two years and is just discovering a positive transference to the therapist, of which the therapist is barely aware and is therefore unable to work with in a functional manner. This is causing him a number of problems.

> The client opens the door and gives me a friendly smile as she turns around to remove her fur coat to place it on a hanger. She turns again and tells me that she has a new fur coat and don't I think it's lovely
>
> The therapist extends his hand, carefully touching the fur and says that it's lovely.
>
> Supervisor one month later: Ah, you touch her pubic hair.

This line gave the therapist a shock that made it possible to discuss transference issues in an entirely new way during the following period. The problems with positive transference that the therapist was experiencing were also reduced as the transference itself changed. Two years later the therapy ended.

Wittgenstein says, that what is mysterious is not "how" the world is, but "that" it is. "How" is expressed in psi and leaving psi is expressed in "that" it is. This movement also represents humanity's responsibility and creative powers. We create patricide, filicide and matriarchy through transformations from "O" and they become ghosts from the past or the future as a kind of psi-column phenomena. But as we move towards transforming "O" in wholeness, empathy, or love, we find our direction. Such a direction is indicated and created in the transference referred to above. It can be effective when it is felt; it does not need to be verbalized.

4. Myth as a narrative of +/– growth and stagnation/death

Myths are consciousness' own transformations of itself. Or myth is a created image of consciousness or psyche outside of time and place in a special language. Consciousness in itself cannot be acknowledged. It is being. Landscape painters transform the landscape like the eye in looking at it and attributes to it qualities, interprets its colour-play and its significances. Since consciousness at once holds all possible things, hence constituting the limits of the possible, consciousness itself may perhaps best be characterized as possibility, becoming, and creation. In relation to itself, consciousness is always true, good and beautiful. This rarely applies to the manifold contents of consciousness. Rather, the contents of consciousness are knowledge and form and hence an expression of limitations and waste-products. The all-encompassingness of consciousness is expressed in Tibetan Buddhism through the icon of Samantabhadra and Samantabhadri in a deep embrace. The Oedipus myth expresses the so-called normal neurotic consciousness with the occasional lapse into the psychotic part. We all know Oedipus in ourselves and we all fear reacting in ways reminiscent of those in which Oedipus reacted.

Thus a client in his mid-50's dreams:

> A boy is playing with his mother's sex. I watch and grow indignant as her sex opens and it becomes possible to see into the dark depths of the opening. I think you could go blind from looking into the female sex. Offended I go into the next room. I discover that it is the room I lived in as a child. I clearly recognize the sofa-bed. The woman is lying in a room that must be my parents' bedroom, in their double bed. The woman is my wife and the boy is my wife's child from her first marriage.

> I wake up feeling very jealous. I discover that I am repeatedly cast into the feeling of being left out.

In the ensuing dialogue we discuss the dream and all situations where the client has felt left out and where he himself has created the situations in which this feeling of exclusion is felt to be painful. He discovers that there were other options but that the choices he made to feel excluded were right and good. We discuss how blindness is followed by desire and how darkness makes it impossible to see and yet constitutes an opening for creating new things; it makes creativity possible.

When the Oedipus myth can be perceived as an icon of consciousness this is because learning, growth and development—i.e., creativity—are the turning points of the myth. As with all tragedies, dramatization takes place in the Dionysian/Apollonian sphere. The oracle of Delphi said "Know thyself" as Socrates tells us even as he makes it his own guiding ambition. The tragedies were performed as annual celebrations in honour of Dionysus. Oedipus is an illustration of how one unknowingly must go forth on the path to self-knowledge. He does so over and over in this theatrical performance in honour of Dionysus.

Hence this myth also expresses a theory of our capacity for learning since precisely the fact that we desire and reject our parents is what enables us to discover the nature of psychic reality. One might say that our consciousness is constellated through the vitally important relations into which we are bound. The Oedipus myth thus become a didactic model showing us how we develop towards a recognition of being, indicating a path to the insight "that" we are and not purely "what" we are.

Oedipus Rex only arrives at showing "what" we are, what Oedipus is; only in *Oedipus at Colonos* does Oedipus become pure being, discovering "that" he is.

Bion attempts to demonstrate two personality aspects as they appear in general consciousness, terming one the neurotic aspect and the other the psychotic.[29]

The neurotic part is the *path towards "what*-recognition" while the psychotic aspect counteracts any stable acknowledgment of reality or insight into "what" you are. In the recognition of the fact "that" you are or in an experience of being-in-oneself the masks of personality dissolves, the ego disappears , the neurotic search for security evaporates, and consciousness comes into its own as an infinite space. The psychotic mode is clearly observable in people who are stable in their psychosis and is characterised by identification of consciousness with its contents. Here the person becomes a "what", i.e., a kind of thing. Attention is not on consciousness with its contents but purely on the contents. Most people know this from themselves, at least partly in the form of being "seized" by madness. This happens when we are subject to collective mass-psychotic states of unconsciousness as with war-psychoses or ethnic psychoses, or individually in the form of infatuation, certain forms of jealousy, rage, and loss of control in extreme violence. There is no doubt that such states are caused by different forms and degrees of anxiety.

The strange psychotic form of insight into a kind of pure "being" untouched by any form of anxiety, will, or influence from the neurotic personality part, is probably what was previously referred to as the mystic beholding of being. The path here is mentioned by St. John of the Cross as the dark night of the soul and the final station of this path can probably only be described as beholding "God"; a "beholding", which obviously cannot be subject to description or conceptualisation.

Bion claims that attacks on "at-states" by psychotic personality aspects are described in a series of myths, with particular reference to the myth of the Garden of Eden, the Tower of Babel, of Oedipus, and of the death of Palinurus in the *Aeneid*.

This does not mean becoming psychotic in the diagnostic sense, but rather of the psychotic personality part staging an attack on our recognition of reality, momentarily robbing us of the possibility of testing reality. Only if these attacks are successful to the extent of overpowering the normal personality section do we become diagnostically psychotic. It can then become difficult to escape the madness and occasionally this cannot take place without lasting damage, so that it becomes impossible to trust that we believe and believe what we know. When this trust is there, however, we let our consciousness stray in an oedipal manner in search of knowledge and mastery of the world. It is this seeking state, which is characterized by the Oedipus myth, and that Bion terms transformations in K.

Psychoanalytic work consists of repeating such transformations again and again, but the goal of the work is to become "O", that is to be oneself, to be one's own truth or existence.

The psychoanalytic concept of "opposition" attempts to express the manipulations of the neurotic part of the personality in order to avoid a collapse of the ego in this last movement towards "O".

The myth of the Garden of Eden is an icon for or describes consciousness in its "O" condition. Prior to original sin, Adam and Eve live in this real existence, but it is an unstable condition, for there is a serpent in paradise. Stability is contingent on the two famous trees in the garden, the Tree of Knowledge and the Tree of Life, are left untouched. The Tree of Knowledge gives access to knowledge "of" or "what" and the Tree of Life gives access to the knowledge "that". The fruit of the Tree of Knowledge crystallises knowledge of elements of existence in consciousness: sex, power, anxiety and later fear, suffering, faith, doubt and finally work and procreation with its efforts, difficulties, and brief joys. This knowledge of the world so that it appears as the contents of life, the "what" of life, was grabbed by our ancestors. But the Tree of Life gives access to consciousness itself, the wellspring of life and creativity or of the essence of life and this was not appropriated by Adam and Eve.

Our ur-parents appropriated this knowledge of the world from the one tree appearing as the contents of existence. Adam and Eve do not acquire knowledge of consciousness itself as the source of life and creativity or the essence of life. Access to this knowledge and the states flowing as fruits from the tree of life is guarded by the zealous God. The cherubs are gruesome guardians of this threshold, preventing all possibility of acquisition and blocking all possible avenues of return to the Garden of Eden where the fruits of the tree of life hang ready to be picked and eaten.

The reason the zealous, almighty, all-knowing God prevents life—blocking access to this tree that also imparts life—seems destined to remain a mystery.

In the language of psychoanalytic myth this God becomes identical with resistance, distortion, repression etc., and hence with a force preventing any actual growth or change in consciousness.

This same insight is expressed in the myth of the Tower of Babel. The people who come together to build a tower to reach God express the attempts of consciousness to reach God at his level through the accumulation of knowledge—what Bion would term transformations in "K"—crossing the threshold to the Tree of Life. The consequences, however, are fatal. Consciousness is smashed to smithereens, its parts dispersed into the infinite void of conscious space with no apparent possibility of being reunited. Consciousness is described as being fragmented into parts with no capacity for mutual communication. The different parts do not speak the same language. Whereas the consequences in the myth of the Garden of Eden almost appear to describe the mode of functioning of the neurotic aspect of consciousness, the myth of the Tower of Babel seems rather to describe that of the psychotic aspect. Here the cohesive force of consciousness is subjected to a far more radical attack, just as the attempts to reach God in order to acquire the essence of life seem to be laid out as if according to a far more coordinated plan.

Perhaps then, these two myths also describe evolutionary states in a form of development of consciousness. The closer and more eagerly we approach "O", the more violent the attacks mounted by the psychotic aspect of consciousness in all its obscurity.

When consciousness identifies with the divine, i.e., when we are in a state of grandiosely inflated madness dominated by the psychotic state, this means that our ability for thought is flawed. A similar flaw is described in the myth of the Garden of Eden as the fragmentation and polarization between the male and the female clearly evidenced in the fact that God "put enmity between thee and the woman, and between thy seed and her Seed; It shall bruise thy head, and thou shalt bruise His heel" (*Genesis* 3:15).[30]

These forms of fragmentation are more comprehensively described in the extensive crypticon of the Oedipus myth as laid out by Lévi-Strauss.[31] Like the classical interpretation of dreams, Lévi-Strauss' interpretation emphasizes condensation, displacement, symbolisation, dramatisation and secondary elaboration (Lévi-Strauss, 1972; Sharpe ,1978).

Based on this schema, Lévi-Strauss claims that the decisive problem of this myth is autochthony vis-à-vis bisexual fertilisation. This myth poses and answers the question of where we come from and who we are. He points out that Freud's use of the myth expresses the same problem without the mythological garb, since for Freud the problem is merely how one can be born of two or in other words: the polarity of fatherhood and motherhood as expressed in the child.

Overestimating blood ties. Excessive intimacy	Underestimating blood ties. Too little intimacy	Killing monsters	Difficulties walking upright
Cadmus seeks his sister Europa, who has been taken by Zeus			
		Cadmus kills the dragon	
	Spartans kill each other		
			Labdacus (Laius' father) = lamb
	Oedipus kills his father Laius		
		Oedipus kills the Sphinx	
			Oedipus = club foot
Oedipus marries his mother Iocasta			
		Eteocles kills his brother Polynices	
Antigone buries her brother Polynices			

Figure 4.3. Lévi-Strauss' schematisation of the Oedipus myth (Lévi-Strauss, 1972, p. 214).

Narcissism and autochthony or relationisation and polarisation. Unity, duality or multiplicity. Thesis—antithesis—synthesis. What is an encounter and how is such a thing even possible?

By the way: this problem has not been solved although our present-day fertility clinics combined with the chemistry of DNA and genetic manipulation techniques appear to have complete control of the workings of fertility or growth.

Understanding of the myth in the structuralist interpretation of Lévi-Strauss arises through understanding the significance of the internal relations of the various columns.

The elements of the last row hold a shared meaning associated with the difficulties in walking upright. Mythologically speaking, Lévi-Strauss thus refers to the fact that all creatures born of the earth have difficulty walking or do so in a clumsy manner. The mythological elements of the fourth column thus claim that people arise by being born of the earth. Man originates from the great mother or Gaia. In the third row, Cadmus and Oedipus kill monsters born of the earth. In other words the facto of being born of the earth is denied. Thus it is clear that rows three and four are contradictory. People are of the earth, people are not of the earth.

These two rows then are to each other as the first two rows, where we see connections with a strong insistence on the ties of blood in row one and disavowal or destruction of this connection since blood relatives kill one another in row two.

This myth is binocular, focusing on opposites and polarities as the psyche that invents it. The myth reflects the space and contents of the psyche. The myth is the sphinx, posing the sphinx's question. At the same time it is the answer: man—psyche—"self-desire"—"who-am-I-desire".

Bion would express this by referring to the urge for truth or humanity's fundamental expression—or being.

If we are to express this interpretation in a more general or abstract manner we might say that the myth asks where creativity lies; in the earth or in the meetings of people; in love and ineptitude or in aggression, anger and hatred. What is creativity? When does it go wrong? What are encounter? Are encounters possible at all?

This question is basically also posed in the interpretations focusing on myth, on the main part of the Attic drama as a verbalization of the conflict between matriarchy and patriarchy or matri- vs.

patrilinearity. This is not only about power, but about encounters and creation—creativity.

The myth expresses this polarity in a number of ways that I shall attempt to paraphrase anew in the following. *Oedipus Rex* is tragic because the poles fail to meet, because these encounters are barren or parasitic. There is no synthesis, synergy or *coniunctio*.

On the surface Oedipus appears to be a description of ontogenetic development from a masculine point of view, where the female responsibility for development is downplayed and suppressed. The tragedy ends in sterility and death for Cadmus' line since all Oedipus' children die childless.

Logos or the Apollonian rationalism becomes dominantly significant. This is the Apollonian oracle informing us of the entire destiny through its repeated prophecies concerning the fates of Laius and Oedipus with the father-son relation as the driving force of this destiny. Oedipus is a tragic figure since he is incapable of transforming the matriarchal principle. His colossal efforts in the form of the investigation he instigates creates no change. It may reveal the mechanisms through which matriarchal power enforces itself, but the release that takes place through the investigative labours of Oedipus uphold the matrilinear principle since Creon—Iocasta's brother—takes over as king after Oedipus. The Apollonian rationalist principle is incapable of producing a creative encounter. The connection between Iocasta and Oedipus is counter-productive or sterile. There are no grandchildren. It creates death. Thebes is struck by the plague. There is not growth but decline and the encounter ends with suicide and self-mutilation.

Remember that the autochthonous theme was described as disastrous at an early stage in Hera's decision to impregnate herself in protest against Zeus bearing Athene after swallowing her pregnant mother. Hera bore the terrible monster Typhon that she gave the oracle at Delphi to raise. He was killed by Apollo when he took his seat at Delphi, but Apollo also had to share his place—although this is frequently forgotten—with Dionysus as well as with Typhon who is buried beneath Delphi and emits up the fumes that send the priestess Pythia into her predictive trance. The fates of Laius and Oedipus are thus determined by poisonous fumes from the great mother Hera's unruly and only begotten son, Typhon.[32]

Sophocles' early work *Oedipus Rex* emphasizes Laius' and Iocasta's shared responsibility for abandoning and maiming their child, and washing their hands of parenthood. They refuse maturity with its ensuing insight into the fact that the time must come for renewal. The baby—an omen of the inevitable impotence of age—is maimed and exposed on the hills of Cithaeron as a beta element. The new principle or renewal of the unconditional love that every baby poses as a possibility is denied. The hills of Cithaeron are like a beta screen onto which this emotional option is repelled. They choose "non-growth" and remain in their barren relation of dependency with power, position and affluence as their main foci. It is a parasitic relationship. Their shared emotion is anxiety; the anxiety of loss, a kind of paranoia that logically creates a field of splitting and schizoid states. The baby is exposed, but saved by shepherds who later become the favoured Christian symbol of Antiquity.

Oedipus Rex ends with the self-blinding and exile of Oedipus, Iocasta takes her own life, her brother Creon takes over Thebes and the city remains under matrilinear power. This means that the psyche continues to be dominated by the feminine. The new has been exiled, fertilisation has failed. Revisiting Lévi-Strauss' columns they show that what does not unite the principles of masculinity and femininity in true bisexual procreation is doomed to be crippled. Thus we all wander without being upright; our club feet on mother earth. We are nailed to the arms of the cross, to the arms of the great mother. *Oedipus Rex* also demonstrates creativity as a possibility in the father's dying for the son, i.e., in the disappearance of the old in favour of the new. However, this happens in a schizoid manner emanating from hate and narcissistic rage over the basic creative conditions of abandonment and death. This happens not through the blessing and forgiveness of the father and the gratitude of the son; instead the attempt is aborted, and this is what is expressed in *Oedipus Rex*; herein lies its tragedy.

What oracle is making this judgement on Oedipus and on us all? What is the Delphic oracle? The oracle demands that we should know ourselves as Oedipus attempts to do with fatal consequences in his investigations of the causes of the plague in Thebes. To Apollo, know thyself means acknowledging his humanity and mortality and dissimilarity to the gods in every respect. But

Dionysus also rules in Delphi. The Dionysian principle stands in opposition to the Apollonian. Dionysus sees humanity as equal to the gods. Man has a nucleus of divinity in the ability to create and love.

Pythia is a chthonic divinity, a god of the earth whose mythological roots reach back into ancient times where the great mother Gaia ruled. Pythia's statements are put forth in a trance after the consumption of hallucinatory substances. Pythia sends Oedipus and Laius back into the arms of Iocasta; Oedipus in Iocasta's bed and Laius in the ground, i.e., in the great chthonic mother at the crossroads, casting her magic spells on them. This enchantment is their destiny. Pythia was a kind of snake born of Hera in protest against Zeus' un-gendered babies—that is to say children parented without the direct involvement of a woman—as well as all his children by women other than Hera herself. Pythia was a monster, banished to the underground beneath Delphi and killed by Apollo in order to live here in the city of Dionysus. The two share the place, but Pythia remains the hidden ruler through the priestesses' predictive trances. These predictions maintain the autochthonous exactly as we see it in *Oedipus Rex*.

The paradigme of Apollo is insufficient, even in Sophocles' interpretation in *Oedipus Rex*. The meeting he secures nails mother and son to one another in a sterile bond, and plague and death ensue. Oedipus' search for knowledge is destined to find truth as well as sterility. The psyche that does not seek challenges in the great foreign void, does not leave mother and father, finds nothing, creates nothing but is destroyed in psi or lies.

This myth displays and explains the connections or structure of such a psyche or consciousness. It is a kind of holographic image of a certain mode of consciousness as well as an indication of a direction in which such consciousness can be changed.

We may regard the myth as narrated by Sophocles as a kind of dream, which also seems to be Lévi-Strauss' view. Thus all the individual elements can be seen as an image or description of a connected psychic reality or the real contents of a structured consciousness. This applies not only at the personal level, but at the collective level too. Thus it may be understood as an image of societal or collective reality and the myth becomes a kind of cultural reality—a sort of image of collective consciousness.

Splitting and opposition is a recurring theme: Oedipus flees his parents in Corinth but approaches them in Thebes. Oedipus' motive is to protect his parents, but the reality is that he kills his father and makes his mother commit suicide. Oedipus seeks Iocasta's help and is warned by her. He seeks help to find the truth through Tiresias, who also warns him. Both know the punishment that will befall those who come too close to the truth. Oedipus helps rid Thebes of the plague but also calls down the plague upon the town. It is as though Oedipus sees things as they are, yet does not know them. He knows without knowing. He sees Laius without knowing him, sees Iocasta, but does not know her as his mother and is forced to "know" her as his wife.[33] Oedipus sees the sphinx and reveals its secret, but he does not see that the sphinx is also like himself and that the secret is as himself. The sphinx as Oedipus' self is as the crippled image of his failed mother and father—who exposed him to certain death in the wilderness through anxiety and fear—that he carries in him. These parents are an internal "bizarre object". The strength of their image paralyzes Oedipus in his search for insight and he crashes into the darkness of unconsciousness precisely like the sphinx. From here the sphinx or "bizarre object" continues its destructive control of Oedipus. This destructivity becomes apparent in the madness, grandiosity and rage that seize Oedipus, e.g., in his encounters with Laius and Tiresias, and with Creon when he returns from Delphi with the message that Laius' murderer must be found. The sphinx is an icon of the psychotic part of the psyche. The paradox is that knowledge of this secret means becoming removed from being oneself. In trying to meet Apollo's demands to know himself, Oedipus becomes removed from himself. The path of Apollo is a blind alley.

Apollo's plot both constructs and destructs the truth of Oedipus and humanity. God's punishment inevitably strikes those that meet his demands.

The myths of the Garden of Eden and the Tower of Babel are icons or tales of consciousness fragmenting or attacking itself; and as in the stories of the sphinx, of Oedipus and Delphi, destruction ensues.

This truth is the truth of consciousness itself formulated in the language of consciousness.

A number of other languages also formulate images of the contents of consciousness. In neurology, psychiatry and neuropsychology a series of metaphors are expressed for selected parts of psychic functioning and contents, as also in psychoanalysis. These are theories of "what" and not of "that". Just as the no. 100 is the "what" that in a certain context constitutes "map no. 100 of San Francisco Bay", that is neither "San Francisco Bay" nor "the sea", it "is in" consciousness but is not itself consciousness.

The myth of Palinurus is another example of Bion drawing forth an icon of a consciousness controlled by its psychotic aspect, driving consciousness towards fragmentation, destruction, death or oblivion. This is also where we find god—in incomprehensible evil—enforcing his will like a hallucination. Palinurus on his way to Sicily steers his ship—guiding the entire fleet of Aeneas—across a calm, black sea while the others sleep. The god of sleep now takes on the form of Phorbas to tempt Palinurus into taking a nap. Palinurus refuses as he does not wish to betray his honour as a sailor and fail his responsibility to the fleet by sleeping on his watch.

> To whom the yawning pilot, half asleep:
> "Me dost thou bid to trust the treach'rous deep,
> The harlot smiles of her dissembling face,
> And to her faith commit the Trojan race?

Acceptance leads to a loss of consciousness or a destruction of its cognitive waking functions. This denial leads to the God's destruction of Palinurus.

> The god was wroth, and at his temples threw
> A branch in Lethe dipp'd, and drunk with Stygian dew:
> The pilot, vanquish'd by the pow'r divine,
> Soon clos'd his swimming eyes, and lay supine.
> Scarce were his limbs extended at their length,
> The god, insulting with superior strength,
> Fell heavy on him, plung'd him in the sea,
> And, with the stern, the rudder tore away.

We can understand this tale as an image of a consciousness at peace with itself and focused on a reasonable and familiar goal. However, this consciousness may hallucinate in the struggle against bodily temptations thus stiffening in a kind of grandiose denial induced perhaps by these very psychic realities of consciousness. Despite this superior state Palinurus falls victim to himself and the leader of the fleet Aeneas comments:

> Deplor'd his death; and thus his pain express'd:
> "For faith repos'd on seas, and on the flatt'ring sky,
> (Vergil, 1994–2000, Book V, line 870)

Most analysts have probably had to acknowledge in 20/20 hindsight how consciousness has been set aside, particularly through the various forms of "acting out" that may be expressed in anger, humour, sexuality and drowsiness.[34] Similarly, interpretations formulated out of sync with the analysand's capacity for understanding or acceptance may be carried by an inability to withstand this sedation of thought that may emanate from the client's internal objects. The corresponding mythical images are the powerfully sedative drops from the Styx. The ability of consciousness to hallucinate through the transformations that shape Phorbas, and its inability to relate in a constructive fashion to the powers thus appearing, fragment the analytic alliance and its constituent consciousness(es).[35]

5. Oedipus at colonos

Sophocles provides a different image of the psyche in the tale of the further fate of Oedipus in *Oedipus at Colonos* where he haltingly seeks to draw in another "vertex" dominated by sensed reality and compassion. This drama is saturated by deep-felt sadness at the misery of earthly existence, but at the same time it is consoling and full of hope for potential change. The turn Oedipus' life takes towards the end also holds an intimation of a possible turn for psychoanalysis. The new notes also herald, as James Hillman has explained, the chords that can move psychoanalysis forward (Hillman, 1991). The new Oedipus has fallen out of the sense of pure sight for he has gouged out his eyes. Blinded, he must refer to his other senses; gaining "insight" through smells, sounds and feel/touch. The song of the birds, the scent of the flowers, the touch and proximity of his daughter Antigone, these are his bearings in the world. He exists in the present moment through these senses. His companion is the sister/daughter figure, rather than the mother or woman. Released from the struggle for power and domination, his death and salvation are secured by his companion Theseus who shares a similar but milder experience. Theseus too was the unwilling and partly innocent occasion of his father, Aegeus' death, having forgotten to exchange his black sails for white before sailing into Athens, the agreed-upon signal that he was alive. Aegeus saw the black sails of the ship and threw himself into the ocean from the top of Cape Sunion, erroneously believing his son to be dead.

It is interesting to note that Freud considered psychoanalysis an instrument for dismantling the Oedipus complex. In his drama on the death of Oedipus, Sophocles himself dismantles the self-same complex he described in *Oedipus Rex*. Insight dominated by sight and the Apollonian rational are exchanged for insight obtained through the other senses and through an inclusion of the Dionysian. Touch, hearing and smell remain, as does the creative nucleus of humanity. Not until the Apollonian combines with the Dionysian to form emotionally sensing thought will such wholeness arise as promises true creativity. The unity of body and thought offers the possibility of truth. Father-mother and sister-daughter love and the love of friendship replace the urge for power and procreation. Theseus' fondness for the old father in his misery opens to the new. Precisely as in Homer's story of Achilles and Priam, whose encounters enable the burial of and posthumous reconciliation with Hector. Analysis as an intellectual exercise has been conquered. Its character of an intellectual ability is considered the illness rather than the cure. The encounters through love, respect and openness that may also constitute psychoanalysis or therapy move in to replace it. Oedipus also achieves complete openness in his encounter with death in a sacred and completely secret place that remains black, dark and entirely unknown to all. This is a place that I presume is reminiscent of Bion's "O" and Milton's indescribable, empty and infinite void, where creation takes place. I think this place and this "O" are the moments in which therapy succeeds: *coniunctio* in matters large, small and frequently unnoticed.

6. Homo oedipus

The stories of Oedipus display the gravitas of humanness. These tales and the others we have discussed here may be understood as a kind of fractals of human consciousness. Unity and detail reveal the same pattern, the same image of a dialectic form that is perhaps inevitable yet indicates a path forward in a Sisyphean struggle. Focus is on the "resistant" Oedipus, who denies his conditions in omnipotent madness and attempts to dominate and control through his ill-conceived desire to "know". He ends up in a kind of self-damaging paranoid-schizoid madness with his world shattered around him. We know this "resistant" Oedipus from analysis, when psychic anxiety and pain play their games with clients and therapists alike. No matter how much we name it in attempted self-defence, it is there, as splitting, pathological projective identifications, acting out, somatisation and—when grandiosity takes the form of meta-theorizing, wild interpretations, cloying sympathy or, understanding and projects on behalf of ourselves or society.

We might say that the form of sexuality we know today is absent in these narratives and in the Oedipus-myth, where sex is not verbalized or ascribed any significance apart from the necessary exercise of power: Children must be begotten and life must be lived, gleaning its status from family and collectivity.[36]

Perhaps the explanation of this difference could be that the specific form sexuality seems to take in our society suppresses the absolute openness and compassion of consciousness. This happens through the psychotic manner of thought characteristic of our time, where scarcity, suffering and misery are constantly in focus because our consciousness is filled with a form of material tyranny where insatiability is the indomitable "what"-content. Sexuality has become an instrument of power in the maintenance of this condition. Aphrodite must be furious!

There is a peculiar irony in the fact that Freud's analysis of sexuality—intended to increase humanity's chance of love and freedom—may itself constitute a part of societal life in a manner that promotes the very pattern it was intended to prevent.

Psychoanalysis, nuclear physics, science, perhaps all the results of our collected labours of consciousness cannot ensure the good, the true and the beautiful. This can only be done through continued labours of consciousness, i.e., by intentionally keeping our consciousness open, containing and compassionate. We must always wonder.

Notes

1. See also Bohr's correspondence with Einstein, 1944.
2. The Hippocratic oath and First Corinthians, 13, 4–8. See also Lambert 1994.

3. In the *Symposium* Plato lets Aristophanes formulate the preconditions of an object-relation theory in the scientific language of the day through the myth of the origins of man as a hermaphrodite sphere, divided by the gods into a male and a female part, bound to spend eternity seeking to be made whole again: Humanity was, is and will be relational.
4. "Being" as existing, as opposed to being something, e.g., "being a redhead".
5. Bion speaks of a state of reverie, where the mother teaches the child to think and where the analyst actively gives up memory and desire to make space for change in the therapeutic process (Symington 1996, pp. 168 ff).
6. Fordham described this process as an alternation between reintegration and deintegration (Fordham 1976 and 1995).
7. In *Cogitations* (1992) Bion speculates on how the rule of Pythagoras expresses the possible pain of three-way relationships and calls the Rule of Pythagoras "Oedipus". Rules thereby become a mathematical abstraction for growth: Ps<=>D. This rule may be compared to the Sphinx, which also expresses both growth and resistance to same; it is a "bizarre object" (Bion, 1957) since it is an icon of a destructive or regressive unity of male and female, quite unlike the alchemic icon of a fruitful union through coitus or the Buddhist Yab-Yum image of Samantabhadra and Samantabhadri, Yin-Yang etc.
8. See Chapter four, Section b: Myth as a Model for Growth.
9. Cf. Freud's archaeological image from "Constructions in analysis" (1937) (Freud 1950, pp. 359 ff).
10. Please see the previously mentioned baby observations.
11. The Jungians speak of enantiodromia, see Samuels 1985, p. 94.
12. The Oedipus myth expresses that which we have referred to as negative growth, while the legends of Christ and the Buddha as well as *The Symposium* express positive growth. Christ, Buddha and Plato represent what Bion calls a "reversible perspective" on Oedipus. People's angle can then "be" or "be in" a positive or a negative impulse.
13. Perhaps this relation and the functional level it expresses is triadic, but it will not be discussed in depth here. It is not the working alliance in therapy that must be examined, but rather the consequences of the establishment of such an alliance. This means that it is primarily the symbiotic and the parasitic relations that are to be examined.
14. Jung would most likely perceive these beta elements as belonging to the psychoid area, thus neither material nor psychic.
15. For beta elements in the form of somatisations and emotions that have arisen *in utero* as far back as conception, see Piontelli 1992 and

deMause 2002, Chapters one to three; Fordham 1976; and Meltzer et al. 1975.

16. deMause 2002 carefully examines how political and social phenomena are rooted in inadequate processing of emotional difficulties. According to deMause, all kinds of violence—even collective violence—are caused by the betrayal and abuse of foetuses, children and youth.
17. Cf. Bion's "bizarre objects" (1967) or Segal's "symbolic equations" (1988). Storage can turn into somatisations.
18. Or perhaps to a desire for further pollution through psychotropic drugs, pot, alcohol, tobacco or the like.
19. Strangely, the religion of the Australian Aborigines seems to conceptualise matters in the same way (Thorborg and Stengaard 1987).
20. Lambert reviews the analytical approach through a comparison of the concept of love in the Hippocratic oath with First Corinthians, Chapter thirteen. See also Nygren 1953.
21. For discussion of memory vs. recall, please see Chapter two, Section c.
22. The word merry is used to translate the Danish "lalleglad", which has no satisfactory direct translation into English. The connotations sought are that of a derogated and unwarranted happiness; joy in the face of adversity.
23. *First Thessalonians* 5.17–18.
24. Authors unpublished notes.
25. Authors unpublished notes.
26. Allow me to quote Heraclitus, "War is the father of us all, King of all. Some it makes gods, some it makes men, some it makes slaves, some free" (Kirk and Raven 1971, p. 195). The result depends of one's attitude to polarity; be it creative or destructive, be it love or hate, be it towards Ps or towards D in the formula Ps<=>D.
27. Our tendency to link phenomena when we observe them simultaneously. Also ibid, p. 228, myths can be understood as constant conjunctions for describing frequent coincidence of events.
28. Matriarchy is strengthened when sons reproduce with their mothers, thus over-determining the feminine. The Oedipus myth seems also to be an interpretation of a position in consciousness halfway between of the dominant mindforms or vertices of matriarchy and patriarchy.
29. These are linked to Freud's descriptions of primary processes and id, and to secondary processes and ego-driven functions. This matter is too extensive to go into here.
30. I see the serpent as a metaphor for phallic masculinity, such that the enmity between the serpent and the woman mentioned here is seen as enmity between the masculine and the feminine. The polarization

and fragmentation is elaborated in the following verses about the punishments of work and reproduction.

31. The end of fragmentation is described in mysticism and that between the masculine and the feminine in particular in the *Gospel of Thomas*, Logion 22.
32. The myth of Christ also describes him as "only begotten". But Mary's mystical impregnation by the masculine element in the form of the dove neutralises the catastrophe, as does Jesus' surrender to the Father before expiring.
33. In *Genesis* 4.1 the verb "to know" is synonymous with "to have intercourse with".
34. Grinberg has constructed the concept of "counter-projective identification", which is a kind of "falling asleep" in analysis.
35. *Medea* and *The Bacchae* also elucidate the link between grandiose consciousness, on the one hand, and madness or loss of consciousness or fragmentation on the other. The classical ideas of nemesis and hubris probably express the same kind of insight.
36. In Ancient Greece sex was of course present, but in another way than we imagine today. Note e.g., decorations of ceramics that portray sex as play, fun, mischief and enjoyment, rendering it present in as manifold ways as it is today.

CHAPTER FIVE

Conclusion

> There is a great deal more philosophy in spiritual exercises like Socrates' dialogues than in the construction of a philosophical system. The task of dialogue consists essentially in pointing out the limits of language, and its inability to communicate moral and existential experience.
>
> (Hadot, 1995, p. 163)

Freud considered psychoanalysis an instrument with which to disassemble the Oedipus complex, thereby developing the innermost workings of consciousness. However, he considered this as an instrumental science, failing to discover that which he was actually demonstrating, namely that the path forward lay in the person; in himself rather than in science.

Similarly, science itself is not an instrument by which to abolish all evil, famine, and poverty. Rather it is the scientists or the people themselves, who through their way of life, their thinking and their practice, themselves become the path to what is good, true, and beautiful.

As people we may be helpers, but only by making ourselves into a path for others to tread. This is what doctors, philosophers and therapists attempt to do in guiding people through treatment for which responsibility is taken. The initial examination and diagnosis are always only partially true since they must always represent a mere part of the problem and the past. The process, on the other hand, encompasses truth and indicates the path to the future.

Hitler was a neglected child whose Oedipus complex took a schizoid turn. He—and half the world—took that path which lays open to a mind shaped by neglect. The state of being at the mercy of a schizoid Oedipus complex calls down a plague on society resulting in self-mutilation as described in ancient Thebes. In 1933 the Danish politician and scholar of antiquity, Hartvig Frisch, published a book on European history from 1918 to 1933 entitled *Plague over Europe* (Frisch, 1933). Here plague is a metaphor for the subconscious aspects that dominate societies under the reign of tyranny in both its spiritual and societal forms. This is the same situation that Danish poet and author, Villy Sørensen, seeks to describe in his *Tutelary Tales* (Sørensen, 1988) and perhaps the same situation we are moving towards in modernity, when we permit state controls allowing anonymous societal powers to cut to the very bone of our private and working lives.

Perhaps the worst of all is the global situation we are currently staging, where confrontations escalate between different primitive cultural forms originating in places as diverse as the North-American prairie, the deserts of Arab Africa, and the trenches of Europe during the last 1500 years.

Laius—who held power—Oedipus—who seized power—and Creon—who inherited power—represent our in- and external tyrants, above all the "nameless dread" caused by lies and unfreedom. When they rule, plague is indeed upon us.

To lift ourselves out of the cloying embrace of this complex is to elevate ourselves to a new level of consciousness. This is the project Bion seeks to reformulate. Our inheritance obliges us to seek to reformulate it ever and anon.

Understanding growth or the nature of creation appears—in principle—to solve the riddle of creativity. Since we mere humans cannot so much as attach a leaf to a tree, it may appear blasphemous to accept this challenge. The ambition may not so much be to solve the riddle as to point it out, thereby loosening the exaggerated, perhaps even grandiose attitude that often characterizes our modern perceptions. In therapeutic schools, this all too often leads to a self-glorifying and self-promoting attitude, which undoubtedly hampers that very creativity which is to lead us onwards.

Instead I would suggest that psychotherapeutic theorists should give up the fight and join forces to graze the infinite meadows of "O".

Psychoanalysis as both science and therapy will undoubtedly find its place within the new paradigm that will be created in the intersection of hermeneutics, natural science and reformulations of the human values that nurture community between people: kindness, consideration, trust, and gratitude.

Bion was not associated with any particular faith, except perhaps that whose only dogma is an unconditional loyalty to the urge for truth. As such he was both a philosopher and a therapist.

True practitioners of philosophy and psychotherapy attempt to live as a real and true part of the shared consciousness they both are and exist in. This—the only true psychic reality—is eternal and unchangeable and pre-exists the thoughts of humanity. This reality has been given many names through the ages. Humanity must change in order to approach and become one with these thoughts. Humanity must adapt to this true reality. When this succeeds, humanity becomes real. Humanity itself will be discovered as the meaningful and the true.

"Psychoanalysis seen through Bion's eyes is a radical departure from all conceptualizations which preceded him. We have not the slightest hesitation in saying that he is the deepest thinker within psychoanalysis- and this statement does not exclude Freud" (Symington, 1996, p. xii).

REFERENCES

Andersen, L. O. et al. (1997). *Placebo. Historie, Biologi og Effekt*. København: Akademisk Forlag.

Bertelsen, J. (1999). *Bevidsthedens inderste: dzogchen*. Copenhagen: Rosinante.

Bertelsen, J. (2003). *Dzogchenpraksis som Bevidsthedsvidde*. Copenhagen: Rosinante.

Bertelsen, J. (1983). *Højere Bevidsthed*. Copenhagen: Borgen.

Bick, E. (1988) "Child Analysis Today." In *Melanie Klein Today: Developments in Theory and Practice. Volume: Mainly Practice*. Ed. Elizabeth Bott Spillius. Vol. 2. London and New York: Routledge.

Bick, E. (1988). "The Experience of the Skin in Early Object Relations." In *Melanie Klein Today: Developments in Theory and Practice. Volume 1: Mainly Theory*. Ed. Elisabeth Bott Spillius. Vol. 1. London and New York: Routledge.

Bion, W.R. "Differentiation of the Psychotic from the Non-Psychotic." *International Journal of Psychoanalysis* 38 (1975): 206–275.

Bion, W.R. (1961). *Experiences in Groups and Other Papers*. London: Tavistock.

Bion, W.R. (1962). *Learning from Experience*. London: Heinemann Medical Books.

Bion, W. R. (1970). *Attention and Interpretation: A Scientific Approach to Insight in Psycho-Analysis and Groups*. London: Tavistock Publications.

Bion, W.R. (1984). *Transformations*. 1965. London: Karnac Books.

Bion, W.R. (1990). *Brazilian Lectures: Parts 1 and 2*. London: Karnac Books.

Bion, W.R. (1992). *Cogitations*. London: Karnac Books.

Bion, W.R. (1993). *Second Thoughts*. London: Karnac Books.

Blake, W. (1977). *The Complete Poems*. Ed. Alicia Ostriker. London: Penguin.

Bohr, N. (1959). *Atomfysik og menneskelig erkendelse*. Copenhagen: Schulz.

DeMause, L. (2002). *The Emotional Life of Nations*. New York: Other Press.

Donne, J. *The Collected Poems of John Donne*. Ed. Roy Booth. London: Wordsworth.

Eigen, M. (1998). *The Psychoanalytic Mystic*. London: Free Association Books.

Fonagy, P., Schore. A.N. & Stern, D.N. (2006). *Affektregulering i udvikling og psykoterapi*. Ed. Jens Hardy Sørensen. Trans. Dorte Herholdt Silver. Copenhagen: Reitzel.

Fordham, M. (1976). *The Self and Autism*. London: Heinemann Medical Books.

Fordham, M. (1995). *Freud, Jung, Klein—The Fenceless Field. Essays on Psychoanalysis and Analytical Psychology*. Ed. Roger Hobdell. London: Routledge.

Freud, S. (1950). *Collected Papers: Vol. V*. Ed. James Strachey and Ernst Jones. Vol. 5. London: Hogarth Press and the Institute of Psycho-Analysis.

Frisch, H (1933). *Pest over Europa: Bolschevisme—Fascisme—Nazisme*. Copenhagen: H. Koppel.

"Gospel of Thomas Hypertext Interlinear." *Metalogos: The Gospels of Thomas, Philip and Truth*. Mar. 2008. Web. 4 Apr. 2008. <http://http://www.metalog.org/files/th_interlin/th022.html>

Grinberg, L. (1990). *The Goals of Psychoanalysis. Identification, Identity and Supervision*. London: Karnac Books.

Grotstein, J.S. (1981). "Wilfred R. Bion: The Man, the Psychoanalyst, the Mystic. A Perspective on his Life and Works." *Do I Dare Disturb the Universe? A Memorial to Wilfred R. Bion*. By James S. Grotstein. London: Karnac Books.

Grotstein, J.S. (2007). *A Beam of Intense Darkness: Wilfred Bion's Legacy to Psychoanalysis*. London: Karnac Books.

Hadot, P. (1995). *Philosophy as a Way of Life: Spiritual Exercises from Socrates to Foucault*. Ed. Arnold Ira Davidson. Trans. Michael Chase. Blackwell Publishing,

Hartt, F. (1994). *History of Italian Renaissance Art: Painting Sculpture, Architecture*. Ed. David G. Wilkins. 4th ed. New York: Thames & Hudson.

Hillman, J. (1991). "Oedipus Revisited." *Oedipus variations: Studies in Literature and Psychoanalysis*. By Karl Kerenyi and James Hillman. New York: Spring Publications.

The Holy Bible, the 21st Century King James Version. Gary, South Dakota: Deuel Enterprises, 1994. *BibleGateway*. Web. 24 Apr. 2008. <http://http://www.biblegateway.com/passage/?book_id=50&chapter=1&version=48>

Johansen, K.F. (1964). *Studier over Platons Parmenides i dens forhold til tidligere platoniske dialoger*. Copenhagen: Munksgaard.

Johansen, K.F. (1991). *Den Europæiske Filosofis Historie*. Copenhagen: Nyt Nordisk Forlag.

Jung, C.G. (1963). *Mysterium Coniunctionis: An Inquiry into the Separation and Synthesis of Psychic Opposites in Alchemy*. London: Routledge.

Kierkegaard, S. (1925). *Samlede Værker*. Copenhagen.

Kierkegaard, S. (1964). *Philosophiske Smuler med afsluttende uvidenskabeligt Efterskrift Udg. i Efterskriftens Hundredaar*. Copenhagen: Hagerup.

Kierkegaard, S.A. (2006). *Fear and Trembling*. Ed. C. Stephen Evans and Sylvia Walsh. Trans. Sylvia Walsh. Cambridge: Cambridge University Press.

Kirk, G.S. & Raven, J.E. (1971). *The Presocratic Philosophers*. 1957. Cambridge: Cambridge University Press.

Klein, M. (1975). *The Writings of Melanie Klein*. Vol. 3. London: Hogarth Press.

Lambert, K. (1981). *Analysis, Repair and Individuation*. 1981. London: Karnac Books.

Langer, M. (1989). *Merleau-Ponty's Phenomenology of Perception: A Guide and Commentary*. London: Macmillan Press.

Levine, P.A. (1998). *Væk tigeren*. Trans. Frank Robert Pedersen. Copenhagen: Borgen.

Lévi-Strauss, C. (1972). *Structural Anthropology*. London: Penguin University Books.

Lévy-Bruhl, L. (1926). *How Natives Think*. Trans. Lillian A. Clare. London: George Allen & Unwin.

López-Corvo, R.E. (2005). *The Dictionary of the Work of W.R. Bion*. London: Karnac Books.

McKirahan, R.D. (1994). *Philosophy Before Socrates: An Introduction with Texts and Commentary*. Indianapolis: Hackett Publishing.
Mejer, J. (1971). *Filosofferne før Sokrates*. Copenhagen: Munksgaard.
Meltzer, D. (1970). *The Psycho-Analytic Process*. Strath Tay: Clunie.
Meltzer, D. et al. (1975). *Explorations in Autism: A Psychoanalytic Study*. Strath Tay: Clunie Press.
Meltzer, D. (1986). *Dream Life: Re-examination of the Psychoanalytical Theory and Techniques*. Strath Tay: Clunie.
Meltzer, D. & Harris Williams, M. (1988). *The Apprehension of Beauty: The Role of Aesthetic Conflict in Development, Art and Violence*. Strath Tay: Clunie Press.
Merleau-Ponty, M. *Phenomenology of Perception*. (1972). Trans. Colin Smith. London: Routledge and Kegan Paul.
Merleau-Ponty, M. (1969). *Tegn. Udvalgte Essays*. Copenhagen: Rhodos.
Miller, L. et al. eds. (1989). *Closely Observed Infants*. London: Duckworth & Co.
Milton, J. *Paradise Lost*. (2007). Ed. Barbara Kiefer Lewalski. 1674. London: Blackwell Publishing.
Myskja, A. (2005). *Musik som medicin*. Copenhagen: Borgen.
Neumann, E. (1972). *The Great Mother*. Trans. Ralph Manheim. Princeton, NJ: Princeton University Press.
Neumann, E. (1995). *The Origins and History of Consciousness*. Trans. R.F.C. Hull. Princeton, NJ: Princeton University Press.
Nygren, A. (1982). *Agape and Eros: A Study of the Christian Idea of Love*. Trans. A.G. Herbert. 1930–1936. Chicago: University of Chicago Press.
Pérez-Sánchez, M. (1990). *Baby Observation: Emotional Relationships During the First Year of Life*. Perthshire: Clunie Press.
Piontelli, A. (1992). *From Fetus to Child. An Observational and Psychoanalytic Study*. London: Routledge.
Plato. *Phaedrus*. (2005). London: Penguin.
Rinpoche, T.U. (1995). *Rainbow Painting. A Collection of Miscellaneous Aspects of Development and Completion*. Ed. Kerry Moran. Trans. Erik Pema Kunsang. Boudhanath. Hong Kong and Aarhus.
Samuels, A. (1985). *Jung and the Post-Jungians*. London: Tavistock/Routledge.
Searles, H.F. (1986). *Countertransference and Related Subjects*. New York: International Universities Press.

Segal, H. (1988). "Notes on Symbol Formation." *Melanie Klein Today: Developments in Theory and Practice. Volume 1: Mainly Theory*. Ed. Elisabeth Bott Spillius. Vol. 1. London and New York: Routledge.

Sharpe, E.F. (1937/1988). *Dream Analysis: A Practical Handbook of Psychoanalysis*. London: Karnac.

Spielrein, S. (1994). "Destruction as the Cause of Coming into Being." *Journal of Analytical Psychology* 39.2: 155–186.

Suzuki, D.T. (2008). *Essays in Zen Buddhism (Second Series)*. Taipei: Cheng Wen Publishing Company.

Symington, J. & Symington, N. (1996). *The Clinical Thinking of Wilfred Bion*. London: Karnac Books.

Symington, N. (2007). *A Pattern of Madness*. London: Karnac Books.

Sørensen, V. (1988). *Tutelary Tales*. Trans. Paula Hostrup-Jessen. 1964. Lincoln, NE: University of Nebraska Press.

Theilgaard, A. (1995). "Metaforer i terapiens tjeneste." *Psyke og Logos* 1: 164–173.

Thorborg, L. & Stensgaard, N. *Mennesket og myten—religion og virkelighedsopfattelse i det nordlige Australien*. Copenhagen: Systime.

Vergil. *The Aeneid*. Trans. John Dryden. 29–19 BC / 1697. 1994–2000. *The Internet Classics Archive*. MIT, 1994–2000. Web. 28 Apr. 2008. <http://classics.mit.edu/Virgil/aeneid.5.v.html>

Walsh, T. (1920). *Hispanic Anthology*. New York: G.P. Putnam's Sons. Print. Vol. 4 of *Hispanic Notes and Monographs*. Peninsular Series.

Winnicott, D.W. (1945). "Primitive emotional development." *International Journal of Psychoanalysis* 26: 137–143.

Winnicott, D.W. (1958/2003). *Collected Papers. Through Paediatrics to Psycho-Analysis*. London: Karnac Books.

Wittgenstein, L. (1921). *Tractatus Logico-Philosophicus*. Trans. C.K. Ogden. London: Routledge and Kegan-Paul.

Zeruneith, K. (2002). *Træhesten. Fra Odysseus til Sokrates—en bevidsthedshistorie*. Copenhagen: Gyldendal.

INDEX

www.ingramcontent.com/pod-product-compliance
Ingram Content Group UK Ltd.
Pitfield, Milton Keynes, MK11 3LW, UK
UKHW022025061126
477531UK00002B/34
* 9 7 8 0 3 6 7 3 2 3 3 9 4 *